Activate 2

enquiries into national citizenship

**Pauline Radley
and Anne Knapp**

General editor: Lee Jerome

**INSTITUTE FOR
CITIZENSHIP**

Published in 2002 by:
Nelson Thornes Ltd
Delta Place
27 Bath Road
CHELTENHAM
GL53 7TH
United Kingdom

02 03 04 05 06 / 10 9 8 7 6 5 4 3 2 1

A catalogue record for this book is available from the British Library

ISBN 0 7487 6020 2

Illustrations by Angela Lumley, Bill Piggins and Peters & Zabransky
Page make-up by Clare Park

Printed and bound in China by Sun Fung

Acknowledgements

The Institute for Citizenship and Nelson Thornes have developed the Activate! range of resources to provide a comprehensive response to the national curriculum for Citizenship at key stage 3. Activate! includes the following components:

Teachers Starter File
Textbooks
Teacher resource pack
CD-Rom
On-line case studies

All have been developed in close consultation with teachers and the case studies and Starter File are the results of an extensive two-year pilot project.

The Institute for Citizenship is an independent charitable trust that works to promote informed active citizenship and greater participation in democracy and society. It was established in 1992 by the then Speaker of the House, the Rt Hon. Bernard Weatherill MP. The Institute develops and pilots innovative citizenship education resources, undertakes research and seeks to stimulate debate around citizenship issues. The work of the Institute for Citizenship is made possible through a wide range of local and national partnerships.

For further information visit www.citizen.org.uk

The Institute would like to acknowledge the support of the following organisations:
The Bridge House Estates Trust Fund
The Equitable Charitable Trust
J P Morgan Fleming Educational Trust
Hackney Local Educational Authority
Halton Borough Council

The authors and publishers wish to thank the following for permission to reproduce photographs and other copyright material in this book:

p 4 Rex/Tim Rooke; p 14 Photofusion; p 16 (left) Rex; p 16 (top) Rex; p 16 (middle right) Rex/Mark Campbell; p 16 (bottom right) Rex/Hrbic Simisa; p 17 (top left) Rex/Paul Brown; p 17 (top right) Liverpool Post and Echo; p 17 (bottom left) Photofusion; p 17 (bottom right) Rex; p 22 (top left) Magnum/Martin Parr; p 22 (left) Syndication International; p 22 (top right) The Independent/Tom Pilston; p 22 (middle top) Andes Press Agency; p 22 (middle) Andes Press Agency; p 22 (bottom left) All Sport; p 23 (middle right) Rex/Boccon Gibod; p 23 (bottom right) Martin Parr/Magnum; p 27 Daily Mail/Paul Cousins and Tessa Cunningham; p 30 (top left) Rex; p 30 (bottom left) Rex; p 30 (second bottom on left) Rex; p 31 (top left) Rex/Tony Kyriacqu; p 31 bottom left, Rex/photographer's name please; p 31 (bottom right) Rex; p 32 Rex; p 38 (bottom left) Still Pictures; p 38 (bottom right) Corbis; p 40 (top left) RSPCA; p 40 (top middle) Still Pictures; p 44 (left) Format/Brenda Prince; p 44 (middle) Format/Raissa Page; p 44 (right) Format/Paula Glassman; p 49 (top) Barnardos (copyright 2000); p 50 Advertising Archive.

Every effort has been made to contact copyright holders. The publishers apologise to anyone whose rights have been inadvertently overlooked, and will be happy to rectify any errors or omissions.

Contents

Finding out

Getting all the information

If you are doing a project or investigation it is useful to get information from many different sources and to find different opinions. If you rely on just one or two books, websites or newspapers you run the risk of not being able to see all sides of an issue. Look at the following examples of students who used only a few sources of information. Think about how their investigation will be influenced by their choice of sources.

Investigation: Should we change the Royal Family?

The next six pages are all about this investigation but each double page shows you a different skill.

USEFUL WORDS

Monarch – a King or Queen

Common denominator – something that we all have in common

Press secretary – someone who deals with journalists on behalf of the government

The Establishment – this refers to the group of people and organisations who are supposed to run the country

Republican – someone who does not want a monarchy

Example 1

Robert has spent some time researching this topic and has collected the following information:

(a) '**Monarchs** can serve as extremely useful and reassuring symbols of stability, especially in periods of massive cultural, economic and political change.'

(adapted from Linda Colley in 'Why Mr Blair is wise to support the monarchy', *The Independent*, 11 April 2001)

(b) 'Most supporters of the Monarchy do not argue for more powers to be held by the Monarchy, but for their independence to be maintained, to be a final check on the Houses of Parliament.'

(from 'Should we abolish the Monarchy?', www.ukpol.co.uk)

(c) 'The United Kingdom is now multi-cultural and far more cosmopolitan than it was in 1895, yet the monarchy, along with all its fancy ceremony, allows us to remember that we are an ancient nation ... The monarchy unites us all as British – a **common denominator**, linking all races, all colours and religions, as the Queen is our Queen.'

(adapted from 'In defence of the Monarchy', from *Monarchy*, March 1995)

TASKS

1 Write a short conclusion for each of the examples, based on the information each student has collected.

2 What differences are there between the two investigations?

3 Can you find any additional sources of information that would help in this investigation?

Example 2

Michelle has collected the following information for her project:

(d) 'Alastair Campbell, before becoming Mr Blair's **press secretary**, said in a newspaper column that "idiotic comments" by members of the Royal Family "provide a constant boost to the **republican** cause". He added: "They are fine when they are opening hospitals, when it comes to opening their mouths they get themselves into trouble." '

(extract from 'Blair seeks to holdback the tide of Labour republicanism', *The Times*, 10 April 2001)

(e) 'A lot of people say "but what would you replace the monarchy with?". We say that is not the point ... nothing of course ... we need no leaders, no divine rulers, or presidents telling us how to live our lives.'

(adapted from an interview with Julian White 'Should we abolish the Monarchy?', www.ukpol.co.uk)

(f) 'The Crown's survival reinforces the impression that British society is shaped like a pyramid and that, at its apex, birth counts for more than merit. This is the greatest contradiction within the British monarchy: every government since World War 2 has said they are committed to equal opportunities, yet here is an institution that shamelessly shows, at the heart of **the Establishment**, nothing has changed.'

(adapted from 'Time for a republic,' *The Independent on Sunday*, 18 February 1996)

TAKING THIS FORWARD

When you research your own projects it is important to take time at the beginning to find as many different sources of information as you can. You can do this easily on the Internet by using a search engine, you can also search some newspaper sites for articles going back several years covering your topic. Remember also that libraries often have easy-to-search catalogues of books and books can be ordered from other libraries for you. Keep a record of the sources you have found.

Justifying opinions

Finding out information is obviously very important, but coming to the right conclusions is just as important. Once you have looked at information about a wide range of facts and thought about the variety of different opinions people have, it is easier to think about your own opinions. The previous two pages looked at two sets of opinions about the monarchy. One selection of sources showed arguments against the monarchy, the other showed arguments in favour of it.

Here are a number of facts and opinions that Robert and Michelle's classmates came up with in their research.

Extra information

(g) 'Monarchy: A form of rule in which there is a single head of state, a monarch, with the title of King (or Queen or some other equivalent). They hold their office for life and occupy the role because of their position in the royal family ... When the monarch rules with full or nearly full powers (in making, applying and judging the law) this is often referred to as an "absolute monarchy". When the powers of the monarch are effectively limited by laws, the system is normally referred to as "constitutional monarchy".'

(adapted from *Glossary of Political Economy Terms*, by Dr Paul Johnson)

(h) 'On almost all matters the Queen acts on the advice of the government of the day. The tasks of making laws, administering justice, and governing and defending the country are carried out by others in the Queen's name.'

(from www.royal.gov.uk)

(i) 'The Queen must agree to all Acts of Law once Parliament has passed them. But no King or Queen has refused permission for a new law since 1707.'

(adapted from www.royal.gov.uk)

(j) 'The Labour Party has not discussed the role of the monarchy at a Party Conference since 1923.'

(from 'Modernising monarchy', *The Guardian*, 10 April 2001)

(k) 'Forty-two per cent of those polled in a recent survey concluded that the monarchy is an expensive luxury that the country can ill afford. Only 34 per cent believed that Britain would be worse off without a monarchy, compared with 77 per cent in 1984.'

(from 'Uneasy lies the head that wears the crown', by Sharmila Devi, 9 July 1996 www.foreignwire.com)

(l) 'The annual figure for the civil list was set by the last Government at £7.9 million in 1990. With Her Majesty the Queen's agreement, and following consultation with the Leader of the Opposition, the Government propose that the annual payment should remain at £7.9 million for the next 10-year period. By the year 2010, therefore, the cost of the Queen's civil list will have remained at exactly the same level for 20 years.'

(Tony Blair, speech to Parliament, 4 July 2000)

(m) 'The Queen is the only person in the country who can dissolve Parliament and therefore start the General Election process. She usually does this when asked by the Prime Minister.'

(adapted from Peter Hennessy in his book *The Prime Minister*)

It seems to me the queen does a useful job, especially as she doesn't get involved in all the political arguments. If she wasn't there to make decisions like dissolving Parliament, who would?

Robert

I do not really like the idea of the Royal Family getting all that money every year, but it's difficult to see who or what could replace the monarch.

Miralee

I can see the argument for a queen or king but the rest of the Royal Family is too big and expensive. Can't we cut down who gets paid and how many palaces they have to live in.

Barry

I think the Royal Family is outdated. We don't need them anymore, especially as we elect our own government to do all the real work and make all the real decisions.

Michelle

Get rid of them.

Josh

It's not the Royals as such I disagree with, it's the old-fashioned ceremonies and all that extra stuff that seems so unnecessary.

Emma

TASKS

1 Select one of the characters and find evidence on this page and the previous pages to support their opinion.

2 Now find some examples of evidence that contradicts their opinion. For each of these, think of an argument that your character might use to defend their opinion.

   e.g. Josh just wants to get rid of the Royals. But Peter Hennessy (source m) points out that the Queen is the only one who can dissolve Parliament. Josh could argue that this doesn't really matter as the job could be given to someone else, for example, the Speaker of the House of Commons.

3 Share your answers with others in the class to see if they can be improved on.

4 Now use all the information to write your own conclusion. Think about your opinion and the evidence you have seen.

5 Look at your conclusion and those from the last page, for Robert and Michelle. Which of the three conclusions is the best?

TAKING THIS FORWARD

Make sure you always try to find evidence to justify your opinions. If you want your opinions to be taken seriously it helps if you can show you have thought about them seriously yourself. Whenever you come to a conclusion in a discussion or piece of written work, think seriously about all the arguments and evidence presented first.

Debating skills

In the last four pages you have been looking at evidence about the monarchy. You have also been thinking about the importance of finding out information from a range of sources and using information to justify your own opinions. You should now be ready to have a whole class debate about the enquiry, 'Should we change the Royal Family?'

To make the debate easier you could decide on one definite idea or proposal to debate – for example:

> The Royal Family should be abolished

Or The Royal Family should be slimmed down so they receive less money

Or We should leave the Royal Family to continue their good job for Britain

Select one of these ideas, or make up your own for the class to debate. This is the motion for your debate.

The diagram shows you the different parts students could play in this debate.

Speaker 1
- Should speak FOR the motion for 3 minutes
- Should also be able to answer questions from the audience
- Should be able to summarise the whole argument FOR the motion at the end of the debate

Speaker 3
- Should speak FOR the motion for 2 minutes
- Should also be able to answer questions from the audience

Audience members
- Listen to the speeches
- Ask questions of the speakers at the end of the speeches
- Make their own contributions – speeches or comments – once the speakers have finished (no longer than 2 minutes)

Chair Person
- Should be fair and firm enough to keep order
- Must explain the motion
- Should introduce the speakers in order
- Should invite people from the audience to make their own speeches or ask questions of the speakers
- Must take a vote on the motion, asking the class to vote, for, against or declare that they are undecided

Speaker 2
- Should speak AGAINST the motion for 3 minutes
- Should also be able to answer questions from the audience
- Should be able to summarise the whole argument AGAINST the motion at the end of the debate

Speaker 4
- Should speak AGAINST the motion for 2 minutes
- Should also be able to answer questions from the audience

TASKS

1 Decide who will take on each of the roles for the debate.

2 Take some time to look through the information on the previous pages and think about the arguments you could use and the points you want to make.

3 Make sure you are clear about the motion – do you support it or not? Would you argue for a different solution? How will you vote?

4 Hold the debate in class.

5 Once the vote has been taken, think about what worked well in the debate. What were you happy with? What could be improved for next time?

TAKING THIS FORWARD

This style of running debates can be used for any subject you are interested in. At the end of each debate try to make time for thinking about how you did and how you could improve. Each time you are preparing for a debate, look back at your previous comments and think about how to improve.

Active citizenship

This book will help you find out about your role as a citizen. It will also help you to understand how you can get involved and help to change things for the better. But a book cannot make you active, you will have to plan what you want to achieve and then work with people to get it done. This section will help you think about how you could do this.

Stage 1
Identify the issue

It will be important to get involved in an issue that you are really interested in. Think about the different issues you come across in the book and in other areas of your school and wider life.

Stage 2
Research the issue

It is important to find out the reasons behind the current situation.

- What is going on?

- How could the situation be improved?

- Who else is involved in the situation?

Stage 4
Action

This could involve setting up meetings or campaigns to put pressure on other people to make decisions for the better. It could also include direct action yourself. For example, setting up local youth groups, helping improve the local environment or establishing a student council.

The main thing is to keep aware of the original aims you had in your plan and to think about how your actions will help you achieve them.

Stage 3
Planning for change

Next you need to think about how you can bring about the change you want. This involves several stages:

- What do you want to achieve?

- Who do you have to work with to achieve this?

- Who are the key people to focus on?

- What actions can you undertake to achieve this change?

- What skills do you and others have to help with the action?

Stage 5
Reflection

It is important to spend some time thinking about how successful any action was. This can help to make it clear how far you met your aims and what obstacles there were. Most importantly it can help to identify lessons for the future. How did you develop your skills and abilities and what do you need to do in the future to improve?

Example of active citizenship in practice

Background

Heath Park Youth Action Against Crime (YAC) was formed in 1991. Over 40 young people aged between 11 and 18 are currently involved in the group. YAC has tackled a wide range of initiatives with support from their coordinating teacher and local Youth Against Crime Officer.

Activities

Projects have included drama competitions; peer-education projects tackling drug misuse; bullying and vandalism-awareness seminars; workshops on these issues and on shop theft.

A link group to local feeder schools has also been established to help new pupils make the transition between schools.

Members also enjoy social activities and day trips during the holidays.

Achievements

A drug-awareness seminar was filmed and broadcast.

A second YAC group (one Junior and one Senior) has been started to accommodate all the students who wished to be involved.

An alcohol support group is planned.

OFSTED inspectors identified YAC's work as being particularly successful.

(example of Heath Park School in 'Partners for Life' from Youth Action Plus)

TASKS

1 Look through the Heath Park example and explain what you think the group's aims were.

2 What actions have they undertaken to affect other people's decisions to help them achieve their aims?

3 What have they done themselves to make a direct improvement?

4 How do you think individual members of YAC may have benefited from their involvement in the group?

5 What skills or abilities would you be able to offer to help a group like YAC?

6 Is there anything that would prevent you from getting involved in such a group?

TAKING THIS FORWARD

Think about what you could do to make a change for the better. Are there groups you could join or would you need to start your own action group? It's important to build in time at the end to think about how well you have done and how you have developed through the action.

Rights and the law: stop and search?

A good police officer will be able to calm a situation and sort out any problems with as little fuss as possible. That's why we are looking for the right people to join our training programme.

What our officers do on the streets affects the way the police service is seen and our ability to work with the community, so we need the right people for the job - a job that is varied and offers good career prospects.

We are looking for people who can help make to their communities safer and better places to live. If you can think on your feet and a looking for a challenge then we can offer you an exciting career with the Framptonshire Police Service.

You must be over 18 years of age, have a good level of general fitness and have good eyesight. You should have a good standard of education and be a good communicator. You should also be willing to work unsociable hours.

TASKS

Look at the picture:

1 In small groups list as many likely reasons why the police might be speaking to these young people as you can.

2 Pick one of the reasons on your list and describe two possible police responses:

(a) First, describe a response that might make the situation worse

(b) Second, describe a response that would help the situation pass without problem.

3 Using the same example, think about two possible responses from the young people:

(a) First, describe a response that might make the situation worse

(b) Second, describe a response that would help the situation pass without problem.

4 Prepare and act out any one of the scenarios you have discussed. Ask others in the class for ideas about how the situation could have been handled differently. Think about what went well and what could have been improved in each situation.

SKILLS FOCUS

- Analysing causes and consequences

USEFUL WORDS

Gender – a person's sex, male or female

Indictable offence – something for which a person can be charged

The law and you

Hello Anita, Simon here. Is that you?

Who else? What do you want?

Why didn't you come last night? I looked for you. You missed a great party. I've still got the hangover.

I think you're pathetic. Fourteen years old and already drunk!

Fifteen — since yesterday. That's what we were celebrating — without you! We started in the pub, not the one we usually go to but that big one on the square. It's really cool there and Mick was spiking my drinks. Then we went to the off licence to pick up the booze for the party. We got cigarettes there as well.

What did your Mum say when she saw all that?

I told you, they've gone to my Gran's for two days. I wouldn't be having the party if they were there, would I? They'll organise another boring party when they get back. Perhaps you'll come to that one?

Perhaps. Anyway, where did you get the money? Won the Lottery again? Another £10?

No. I've got money. There's my wages. I'm not lazy, I've been washing up in the kitchens of 'The Blue Rose Restaurant' for two years now AND my parents gave me £30. I haven't spent it all but I've got plans.

I can imagine.

Yeah. The £30 isn't enough for some decent trainers but I'm going to have a tattoo or get a nose stud. I haven't decided which yet. Then I'll get a passport and go to Spain, do some clubbing, in the summer. Fancy coming along?

I don't think it's my scene.

But the party would have been. We went mad! About three o'clock we were all running through the streets throwing fireworks at one another. It was great!

Mmmmm. Sounds really mature.

You're not cool. Won't you even come for a ride on the motor-scooter when I get it?

In your dreams! Bye!

Anita!

TASKS

1 How many things does Simon describe that could harm his health?

2 How many times has Simon broken the law? Make a list of the things mentioned here that a 15-year-old cannot do legally.

3 What advice, if any, would you give Simon?

The causes of crime

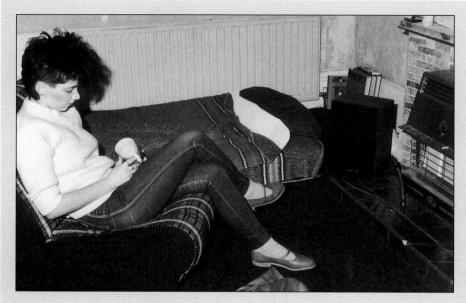

Marie had her usual breakfast of a cigarette and a cup of strong, sweet tea. She fiddled with the button on her blouse; she couldn't relax without a fix and she had not had anything since yesterday afternoon. Where could she get the money from to get what she needed? What if Jason came home and there was nothing for dinner? Another row. He was getting above himself, a 13-year-old boy threatening his own mother. Of course, he didn't come home often now he'd got those new friends. He said they had a flat and let him stay over. Well, it was better for him than this pokey dump with its broken window and the mildew patches in all the rooms. As soon as she'd had a fix or a drink, she would tidy up a bit and make it look a bit more like home.

Marie knew her life should not have been like this. She had been a pretty girl, not bad at school and she had been popular. Her parents had wanted her to be happy and at 14 years old when all the other girls were swotting for their stupid exams, she had gone out and had fun like you are supposed to when you are young.

Craig had been 22 years old when she met him outside the pub, where a gang of people were messing around. He had liked her at once and treated her properly, buying her drinks and taking her places in his car. He had given Marie her first joint. Life had been a dream then! Of course, Craig had taken off when she had told him about the baby, but you could not expect a man to be pleased to find out he was going to have a baby by a 14-year-old girl. It was all her fault anyway. She should have gone on the Pill, but it was all too much bother.

Gary had been such a pretty baby but he grew up into a whining, screaming, dirty little thing who never gave her a moment to herself. He took after his father's family, she supposed. Anyway, he has been nothing but trouble. Of course he had been picked on at school, all the kids from this estate were looked down on, so he had played truant and bunked off with his mates. Free all day and wanting the things she could not afford to give him, he had started shoplifting and then done a bit of burgling. To be fair, he did sometimes give her some money when his luck was in. But that was over now he was in jail again. Four years this time, for robbery.

And now there was all this trouble with Jason. He was too much for her, he needed a man's hand but she was not going to tell that to all the nosey-parker teachers who kept sending for her. They'd soon send the social workers round to poke their noses in. No, Jason was all right, he was just growing up a bit fast and there was nothing for him to do in this dead-end dump. The school didn't even try to teach him anything so why should he go to it? Marie knew she had to go out and get some money somehow and soon. She needed that fix.

ACTIVITY

Jason has been charged with robbery from a nearby house while playing truant from school. Although only 13 years old, he must now appear at the Magistrates Court. Imagine you are the solicitors. Work in pairs to produce the speeches you will make when

(a) defending Jason

(b) accusing Jason and putting the victim's case forward.

Make as many points as possible. Share your ideas with others in the class and make a decision about his case.

Crime: the role of age and gender

Do age or **gender** play any part in the crime rate of Great Britain? The facts and figures given on this page will help you to answer that question.

TASKS

1 Check the sentences below against the table and graph. Are the sentences all correct? Change any that you think are inaccurate.

(a) In 1998, 532,000 people were either found guilty or were cautioned for **indictable offences**.

(b) According to the data, the peak age for offending for males, in 1998, was 18 years.

(c) The graph shows that the peak age for offending for females is older, at 21 years.

(d) The second most common crime committed by males aged 16 to 24 was violence against the person.

(e) The graph shows that males and females are almost equally likely to commit a crime at the age of 65 or over.

(f) The graph shows that at all ages there is little difference between the numbers of men and women committing crimes.

(g) The commonest crime committed by the youngest criminals, both male and female, is the theft and the handling of stolen goods.

(h) The age of criminal responsibility, in England and Wales, is 10 years.

2 Choose two facts that have surprised you. What is so unexpected about them?

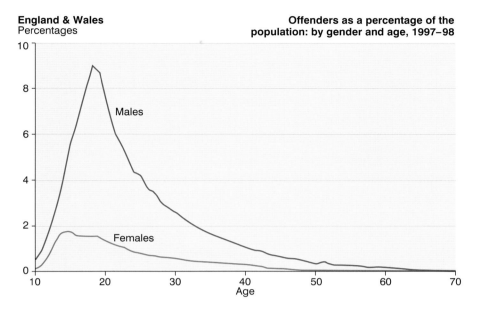

England & Wales
Percentages

Offenders as a percentage of the population: by gender and age, 1997–98

Males

Females

Age

Offenders found guilty of, or cautioned for, indictable offences*: by gender, type of offence and age, 1998

England & Wales   Rates per 10,000 population

	10–15	16–24	25–34	35 and over	All aged 10 and over (thousands)
Males					
Theft and handling stolen goods	133	221	88	18	152.2
Drug offences	15	177	70	9	96.0
Violence against the person	31	74	33	8	51.7
Burglary	40	66	18	2	37.2
Criminal damage	11	18	8	1	12.4
Robbery	6	11	2	–	5.6
Sexual offences	3	4	3	2	5.5
Other indictable offences	11	104	61	12	74.3
All indictable offences	250	674	282	53	435.9
Females					
Theft and handling stolen goods	73	75	30	7	56.8
Drug offences	2	18	10	1	11.5
Violence against the person	11	12	5	1	8.9
Burglary	4	3	1	–	2.0
Criminal damage	1	2	1	–	1.3
Robbery	1	1	–	–	0,6
Sexual offences	–	–	–	–	0.1
Other indictable offences	3	21	13	2	15.0
All indictable offences	95	131	61	12	96.1

* People found guilty or cautioned for indictable offences in 1997–98

Crime: the causes and consequences

Every crime, however petty or unimportant it may seem, has consequences for all of us, even if we are not directly involved. The theft of a pencil from school, for example, may seem harmless but if everyone did it all the time it could lead to cutbacks on other equipment to pay for the replacement of the stolen items. This section should encourage you to think of the many possible consequences of crime and to think about the reasons why people behave in such an anti-social way.

TASKS

Work in groups of four, if possible.

1 Two people should collect all the possible causes of a crime.

2 The other two should work on all the possible consequences of that crime.

Think about the individuals and society as a whole.

3 Join together as a group of four to complete the table on page 17.

4 Now look back over the whole of this chapter and pick one type of crime you are particularly interested in. Try to think of as many ways as possible to reduce the levels of this crime.

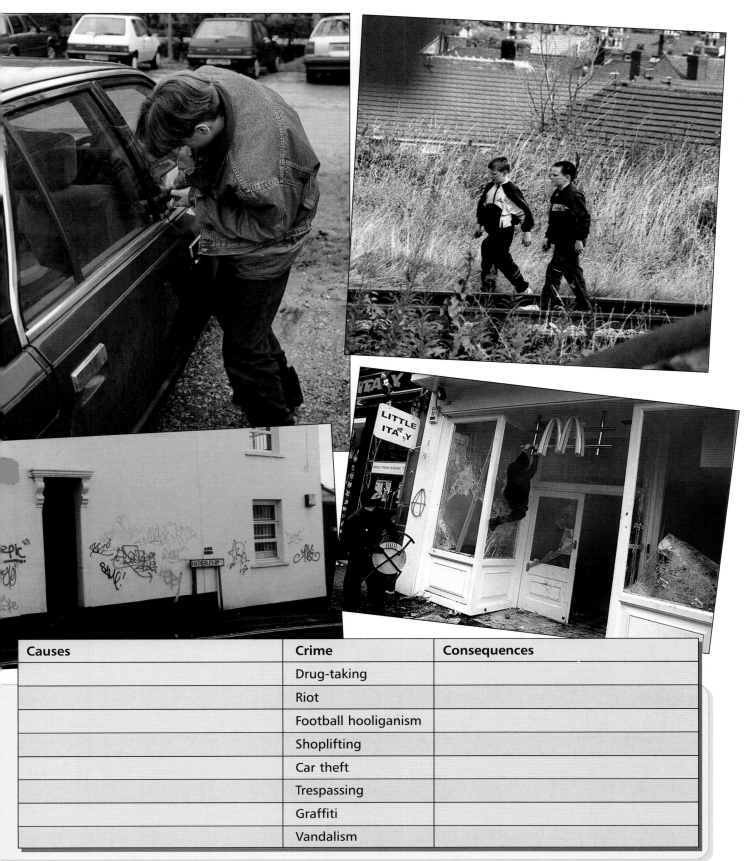

Causes	Crime	Consequences
	Drug-taking	
	Riot	
	Football hooliganism	
	Shoplifting	
	Car theft	
	Trespassing	
	Graffiti	
	Vandalism	

 DIVERSITY

The United Kingdom: four nations into one?

TASKS

1 Divide a page in your exercise book into quarters. Give each quarter a heading for each of the countries that make up the UK.

2 Add the correct flag and population figures.

3 Sort through the statements and facts and figures scattered around these two pages and make notes under each of the headings.

4 On another page of your exercise book, make a heading for the UK. Add a flag and the population figures. What notes can you make about the UK, from using these figures?

SKILLS FOCUS

- Develop and justify your own opinions about what it means to be British

USEFUL WORDS

MP – Member of Parliament. MPs are the elected representatives of the House of Commons

MEP – Member of the European Parliament

(1) Population 49,500,000

(9) Became part of the UK in 1707 as a result of the Act of Union

(15) Capital city – Belfast

(5) Patron Saint – St David

St David's Day is on 1 March

(12) Has always been the largest, most powerful part of the UK

(18) Sends 40 MPs to Westminster and 5 MEPs to the European Parliament

(4) Population 1,700,000

(2) Population 5,100,000

(19) Sends 18 MPs to Westminster and 3 MEPs to the European Parliament

(6) Patron Saint – St Andrew

St Andrew's Day is celebrated on 30 November

(16) Capital city – Cardiff

(3) Population 2,900,000

(10) Became part of the UK in the years 1536–42 after being conquered by England

(14) Capital city – London

(8) Patron Saint – St George

St George's Day is celebrated on 23 April

(20) Sends 72 MPs to Westminster and 8 MEPs to the European Parliament

(7) Patron Saint – St Patrick

St Patrick's Day is celebrated on 17 March

(13) Capital city – Edinburgh

(17) Sends 529 **MPs** to Westminster and 71 **MEPs** to the European Parliament

(11) Became part of the UK in 1921 when the south of the country became independent

SURVEY

Carry out a survey to find out what people know about the UK and what they think about the country they belong to.

Some questions to get started with could be:

- How many countries make up the United Kingdom?

- Which country has Saint Andrew as the patron saint? Etc ...

- Where do most people live within the UK?

- Which do you feel is more important to you, the UK or one of the four nations?

- Should the UK as a whole carry on or should we divide into four separate countries again?

Many nations as one?

In this section you will learn about the many different influences that have combined to form the British people and the English language. The language used by the vast majority of the citizens of Britain is English, which has also become a world language – one person in seven in the world has some knowledge of it.

The development of English

The vocabulary of modern English is made up of words drawn from many languages:

Germanic
'House', 'tree', 'day', and 'come' are examples of words that can still be recognised in German and the Scandinavian languages. Numbers and colours come from the same source.

Latin and Greek
Legal terms are taken from Latin and Greek, as are many scientific terms: for example, 'photosynthesis' and 'thermometer'.

Hindi
'Pyjamas', 'dinghy', 'jungle' and 'thug'.

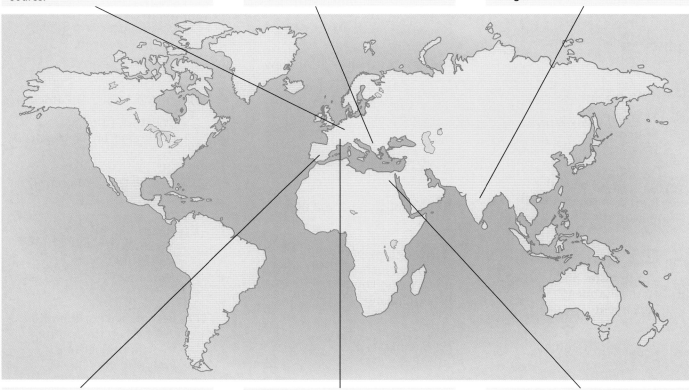

Spanish
'Cigar' and 'potato'.

The Romance languages and Southern European languages
'Robe', 'beef', 'parliament', 'liberty' and 'probability'.

Arabic
'Mosque' and 'zero'.

Facts from previous page:
England 1, 8, 12, 14, 17
Scotland 2, 6, 9, 13, 20
Wales 3, 5, 10, 16, 18
Northern Ireland 4, 7, 11, 15, 19

The spread of English as a world language has been helped by history: Britain had colonies all over the world where English had to be spoken. Also, English is a simple language and people can learn to speak a little of it very quickly. English is the language spoken in the USA, the most powerful nation at the present day. It is also significant that English reflects so much of the other languages of the world; speakers of many other languages can find something familiar in its vocabulary or structure.

Ethnicity: who are the British?

13th century – We Northern Italians were experts in banking. We set up the first banks here.

1000 BC – We Celts came from France and Belgium. We hunted for food here.

1945 – I had nowhere else to go. My homeland in Eastern Europe was destroyed in World War 2.

1950s – We came from the former colonies like India, Pakistan and Bangladesh. We were British subjects and there were jobs here.

AD 43 – We came with the Roman army to conquer Britain and take its minerals. We built too.

1948 – We came from the West Indies to help rebuild Britain after World War 2.

13th century – We came with other Flemish wool merchants to buy and sell wool and develop trade.

19th century – Many of us left Ireland and came here to find work. There were jobs building roads, bridges and railways.

1960s – Many of us came from West Africa because there was racial persecution of Asians there.

8th century – We came from Scandinavia with the other Vikings. We conquered the land and took slaves.

1950s – We left Southern Italy and came to Britain to find work.

1990s – We came from the Balkans, the former Yugoslavia. Many of us had to escape war and persecution.

1066 – We came from Normandy to help our king conquer the land.

1950s – We came from Hong Kong; we had British passports and there was work for us to do here.

1930s – We fled Nazi Germany: they were killing Jews there.

TASKS

1 Make a list of all the countries which have had a big impact on shaping modern Britain. This could be presented as a map, or a display by the whole class.

2 Can you add any other influences from other countries that have influenced how Britain is today? Think about food and drink, music and films.

3 Write up your own timeline to show key events that have influenced modern Britain.

The UK: one nation?

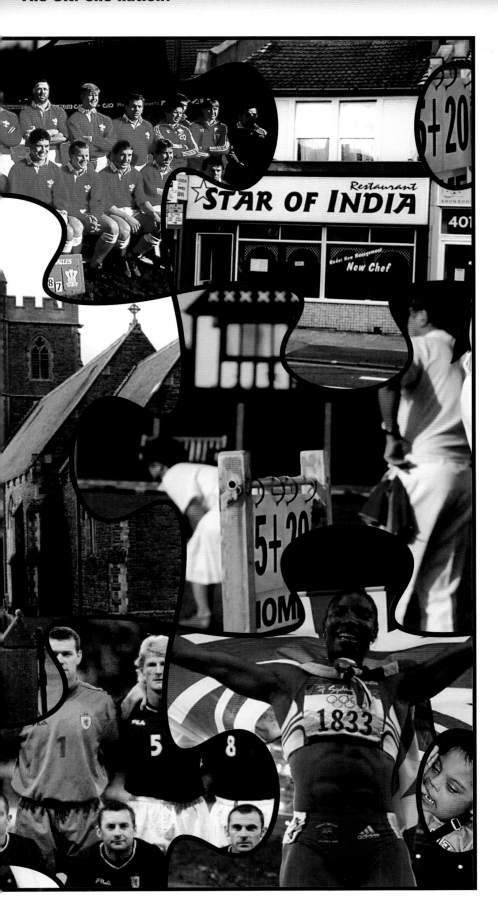

TASKS

1 What elements of British identity does each image show you?

2 What does 'being British' mean to you? Do you agree or disagree with others in your class?

3 What images would you include to show the diversity of Britain? Design your own jigsaw of 'Britishness'.

4 Look back over the rest of this chapter and think about the information presented. How united is the United Kingdom? Remember to weigh up the evidence before you come to a conclusion. Hold a class discussion to explore other people's opinions.

Taxing and spending

This section will tell you something about the way in which the government gets money from the population and how it spends that money. You will have the opportunity to think about financial decisions and their consequences at government level and at more personal levels too.

USEFUL WORDS

Bill – the name given to a draft law before it is passed by parliament. A Bill can change as MPs discuss it; once they accept it, the Bill becomes an Act of Law.

Duties – taxes on certain kinds of products, especially imports

Expenditure – spending

Consumer – customer

Retailer – seller, for example, a shop or catalogue

Taxation: some questions and answers

'Taxes, after all, are the dues that we pay for the privileges of membership in an organised society.'
Franklin D. Roosevelt

'The point to remember is that what the government gives, it must first take away.'
John S. Goldman

TASK

Read the following questions and match them to the correct answers. Make a note of the facts in your exercise book or folder.

1. What is tax?

2. Do all governments take tax?

3. Where does the government take this tax from?

4. What is PAYE?

5. How does the employer know how much to take?

6. Do I pay tax on every penny I earn?

7. Who decides how much tax we should pay?

(a) A minister called the Chancellor of the Exchequer. He discusses the matter with other ministers and prepares the Budget, usually in November, with his plans. These plans then become a **Bill** and are discussed in Parliament.

(b) The money that the government takes to spend on the country and its people.

(c) No. There is a certain amount, called the Personal Allowance, that is not taxed. In the years 2000–2001 that amount is £4,385. After that the rate of taxation begins at 22% of earnings.

(d) The tax office, or the Inland Revenue, works it out and gives the employer a table to work from.

(e) Yes, but different parties have different ideas about how much to take and what to spend it on.

(f) It means Pay As You Earn and is the tax that is taken from wages or income before we get our pay.

(g) The money comes from income (PAYE), from VAT, from the profits of businesses, from the interest on savings and from **duties** on tobacco, petrol, alcohol, etc.

Government spending

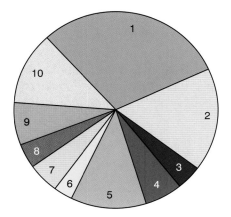

1 30% social security	**6** 3% transport
2 17% health	**7** 5% law and order
3 4% housing/ environment	**8** 4% industry/ agriculture/ employment
4 6% defence	**9** 7% debt interest
5 12% education	**10** 12% other

▲ Government expenditure

TASKS

1 Copy the table into your exercise book or folder. For each budget heading add the areas for which the Government has responsibility, from the following list:

- schools, colleges, teachers
- police, prisons, courts
- roads, rail, air traffic
- factories, farms, and jobs
- medicines, doctors, hospitals
- army, navy, weapons
- rivers, air quality, homes
- help for poor people, families, the unemployed

2 Using the pie chart, add the percentage of total **expenditure** for each.

3 Government expenditure for the period 1999–2000 was £346 billion. Work out the actual amount of money each department spent. Add the information to your table.

4 Do you agree with the government's priorities? Would you spend the money in the same way? If not, what would your priorities be?

5 Imagine no one pays any tax for the next 100 years. Draw a picture or write a description of the scene and the society that might have developed in 100 years' time.

Areas of Government Expenditure	% of total expenditure	Spending (£bn)
Social Security		
Health		
Housing/Environment		
Defence		
Education		
Transport		
Law and Order		
Industry/Agriculture/Employment		
Debt interest		
Other		

A tax on your spending

Value Added Tax (VAT) was introduced into the United Kingdom on 1 April 1973. Originally the rate of tax was 10% but now it is 17.5% on most goods. VAT is basically a tax on spending – that is, it is a tax charged at every point where goods or services are exchanged between the time of their primary production and the time they reach you – the final consumer.

It does not matter how much a person earns as VAT is the same for everyone. However, there are some goods that are zero-rated – that is, the consumer does not have to pay tax on them. The goods which fall into this category are newspapers, books, many food products, and children's clothes and shoes (depending on the size).

TASKS

1 Look at the picture on page 27. Copy the table below and add into column 1 all the items in the picture with a price tag.

2 Use a calculator and the formula below to work out how much VAT you pay on each item.

Formula

$$17.5 \times \frac{\text{cost of product}}{100} = \text{VAT}$$

3 Work out the total cost of goods and the total VAT.

4 Do you think VAT is a fair tax? Explain your answer.

5 If the government did not collect VAT where else would they get the money from to spend on services?

6 Have a debate on the fairest way for governments to raise money. Try to think of the advantages and disadvantages of:

(a) VAT

(b) Income tax

(c) Taxes on petrol, smoking and alcohol

(d) Borrowing

(e) Business tax

(f) Taxing imports to the country

(g) Taxing pollution and energy use

(h) National Insurance (paid by employees and employers

Can you think of any other ways the government could raise the money it needs to spend to keep all its services running?

Item	Price	VAT
1. Trainers	£100	£17.50
2. CDs (40 at £13.99 each)	£559.60	£97.93
3.		
4.		
	Total cost =	Total VAT =

TERRIBLE TWEENS

LAURA'S POSSESSIONS

Portable TV: £90
Video: £140
Portable stereo: £80
20 CDs: £200
Computer with Windows 95, printer and scanner. Shared with James: £1,500
20 books: £100
21 textbooks and revision booklets: £190
Make-up: £90
Collection of shower gels and body moisturisers: £100
Collection of perfumes: £140
Water filter: £20
Pine bed, 4ft 6in, with integral desk: £150
M&S bedspread: £120
Laura Ashley curtains: £80
Three pine chairs: £300
Two pine chests: £450
Telephone: £20
Three teddies: £60
Five pairs of jeans: £150
Six tracksuit bottoms: £180
Ralph Lauren top: £60
12 jumpers: £360

10 T-shirts, mainly Nike and Adidas: £200
Three polo-neck jumpers: £45
Two Ralph Lauren jackets: £90
Ralph Lauren blue hat and scarf: £30
Nine shirts from Kookai and Morgan: £225
Four tops: £120
Three-piece suit: £150
Eight lightweight jackets: £400
Eight tracksuits: £400
Two pairs of sports shorts: £35
One pair of boots: £20
Two pairs of sandals: £30
One pair of pods shoes: £60
Two pairs of trainers: £100
Underwear: £100
Backpack: £20
Jewellery: £120
Ornaments: £90
Polaroid camera: £25
Canon camera: £90
Two watches: £120
Hairdryer: £15
Hair styling brush: £22

TOTAL: £7,087

JAMES'S POSSESSIONS

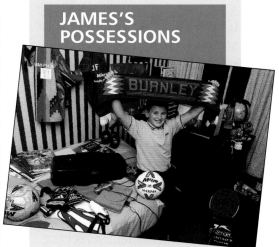

Portable stereo: £80
Personal CD player: £20
Personal tape player: £17
Sony PlayStation: £115
Eight computer games: £240
20 CDs: £200
Designer T-shirts: £125
Three pairs of jeans: £60
Five pairs of trainers: £150
Three tracksuits: £120
Four jumpers: £80
Six coats: £360
Four backpacks: £80
Two pairs of shoes: £90
Five cans of deodorant: £20
Hair gel: £25
Lava lamp: £25
Swatch watch: £60
Casio watch: £50
Single bed: £150
Three duvet covers: £120
Curtains: £50
Chest of drawers: £120
Socks and underwear: £100
100 cycling magazines: £160
15 textbooks and manuals for school: £105

TOTAL: £2,722

EXTENSION TASK

Produce a similar picture for a room in your house. Work out how much VAT, approximately, was paid on the goods in the room. Ask adults at home to guess the amount before you tell them. Do you think they will be surprised when they hear the actual figure?

Taxation and the National Lottery

Lotteries have existed for at least 600 years and the money they raise has been used in a variety of ways: for example, the lottery held in Bruges and Ghent (in modern Belgium) in the 13th century provided funds for the strengthening of the city walls. Some people argue that because the lottery money helps to fund the kinds of services government provides it is like an indirect tax. Others say that the lottery is completely separate and provides extra money for projects the government would not otherwise be able to fund.

In this section you will be asked to think about the National Lottery and its place in our society.

(5) The lottery is democratic and unites people of all types.

(18) Many theatre, dance and leisure groups depend on the lottery grant for their existence.

(8) The government takes 13p of every £1 spent.

(21) Many people no longer see work and a careful attitude to money as a means to prosperity: they believe they can win!

(1) Anyone, rich or poor, can become a millionaire; about 900 people already have!

(12) The budget of the Department of Culture, Media and Sport has fallen from 0.16% of National Income to 0.1%.

(6) The lottery provides money for many good causes.

(15) The sale of lottery tickets is a form of taxation in disguise.

(2) Britain's success in the two Olympic Games in Australia was due, in part, to grants of lottery money.

(25) The lottery is a complex organisation that employs a wide variety of people.

(11) Lottery grants are used to finance important building projects.

(20) People do not give to good causes, they want to get something in return.

(16) The sale of lottery tickets helps keep thousands of newsagents and corner shops in business.

(24) It is difficult to fill in an application for a lottery grant: time, expertise and professional help are needed.

(13) The lottery is equally popular with men and women.

(4) The main charities have received £1 billion less in donations since the lottery began.

(23) Some of the organisers have become very rich without having to buy a lottery ticket.

(7) The government spends less money, leaving it to the lottery grants to provide sports and leisure facilities.

(22) Only 50% of the money received is given back to the participants.

(14) The poor are paying at a higher rate because a bigger percentage of their income is returned to the government.

(9) People in all regions of Britain and of all classes participate equally in the lottery.

(10) The lottery creates jobs and makes the country more prosperous.

(19) There is some dissatisfaction with the way the lottery money is shared out.

(3) Money is often spent on opera, ballet, rowing – that is, on pastimes enjoyed by small groups of rich people.

(17) The National Lottery is turning Britain into a greedy, selfish and lazy country.

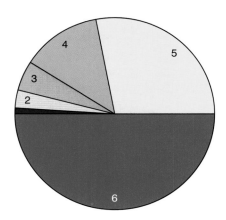

1	1p profit	**4**	13p government
2	3p operating costs	**5**	28p good causes
3	5p retailers	**6**	50p winners

Camelot: Social Report 1999. Social Report Feedback. Camelot Groups plc, Tolpits Lane, Watford, WD1 8RN

▲ **The lottery – where does your pound go?**

TASKS

1 Read the statements about the lottery and sort them into three types:

Statements in favour of the lottery

Statements opposed to the lottery

Statements that are neutral or factual.

2 Are there any changes that you would like to see made in the lottery?

For example, should people under 16 be allowed to play? Do you agree with the way the money is allocated?

3 What do you think of the lottery? Prepare a short speech summarising your own opinion and giving evidence to support the main points.

Imagine you are giving advice to the government about the rules they should set for the lottery operator. What advice would you give them? What changes if any would you want them to introduce? Explain how to improve the lottery.

4 Once everyone has discussed their opinions have a group debate.

Who governs Britain?

SKILLS FOCUS

- Think about the role of individuals and organisations in running the country

USEFUL WORDS

Judiciary – all judges

Court of Appeal – a higher court you can go to in order to have your case reconsidered

Westminster – the area in London where Parliament is located. People often refer to Westminster when they mean Parliament

Constituency – an area that elects one MP; some large towns are divided into several constituencies

Manifesto – the list of promises political parties make before elections about what they will do if they become the next government

TASKS

Arranged around the page are some of the groups and organisations who help to govern Britain.

1 Below are the captions for each of the pictures. Decide which caption fits which picture.

(a) Monarch – has the power to dismiss Parliament and call an election. After the election s/he invites one person to become Prime Minister.

(b) Local government – important in running local services such as waste disposal, roads and schools.

(c) The Cabinet – a meeting of senio Ministers who come together to discuss government business.

(d) Prime Minister – leader of the government; appoints everyone else to run departments.

(e) Courts – they decide what laws actually mean in real situations and can influence the impact of a law.

(f) European Parliament – people are elected from every country in the EU to pass laws which affect everyone.

(g) Members of Parliament (MPs) – each MP represents one local area; they meet together in Parliament to discuss and pass laws.

2 Can you add any other groups or individuals who have a part to play in governing the country? Add them to the list.

3 For each of the items in your list, think about how you and other citizens in the UK can influence them. What methods could you use for each one?

4 Try to find out some more facts about each of the groups in your list, and report them back to the rest of the class. Think about who has most power in government.

Parliament

Parliament is really made up of three parts: the Monarch, the House of Lords and the House of Commons.

The Monarch

The Monarch is Head of State, Head of the Church of England, Head of the Armed Forces and Head of the **Judiciary**. In Britain the Monarch has to follow the advice given by the government of the day. However, the Monarch has a number of important duties such as:

- agreeing to and signing the laws

- opening Parliament

- visiting foreign countries to represent Great Britain.

The House of Lords

The House of Lords has existed since the 14th century and is made up of archbishops, bishops, and peers (lords). They are unelected, unpaid and their attendance at the House is voluntary. There are approximately 800 lords but there is no limit on the number, or on their term of office. Their duties and powers include:

- examining laws and suggesting changes

- slowing down the passing of law

- passing judgement on law cases as the highest **Court of Appeal** in the country.

The House of Commons

This is the most important part of Parliament as the Members are elected by the people for a five-year term. All 659 of them are paid and are expected to attend Parliament to carry out such functions as:

- making laws

- voting for taxes so the Government has the money to carry out its plans

- discussing problems and examining the Government's ideas for solving them.

Inside the House of Commons

The business of the House of Commons begins each day at 2:30pm when the Speaker walks in procession to the House and sits in the Speaker's Chair, a throne-like seat that faces south and gives the Speaker a full view of the chamber, making the job of keeping order easier.

Three Clerks of the House, wearing wigs and black robes, sit directly in front of the Speaker; they are there to advise on the rules of Parliament. In front of the Clerks' desk stands the Table of the House. On the table there are two Dispatch Boxes and the Mace, the symbol of the authority of the House. Front-benchers stand near the Dispatch Boxes when they speak in a debate.

On both sides of the House, there are 5 rows of benches, 437 seats in all. MPs belonging to the party in power sit on the Speaker's right while the Opposition Benches are on the Speaker's left. Important members of both parties sit on the Front Benches, the front row.

Two red stripes run the length of the chamber. They are two sword-lengths apart and were placed there originally to prevent fighting during debates. The space between the benches is marked with a white line at the south end of the chamber, this the Bar of the House and MPs who have been told off have to stand there.

In a democracy, people have the right to know what is being said in their parliament, so in a Gallery, high above and behind the Speaker, sit the Press and, below them, Hansard Reporters, who take down all the speeches in shorthand and publish them by 7:30 on the morning following the debate.

The general public have the right to listen to the debates from the Strangers' Gallery, situated next to the Members' Gallery, where important visitors sit.

TASKS

1 On your own copy of the picture of Parliament, add notes showing all the main people and places underlined in the writing above.

2 Read all the information on these two pages and decide whether the following statements are true or false:

	True	False
(a) Parliament is made up of elected people only.	☐	☐
(b) The Queen has no power.	☐	☐
(c) The general public are kept out of the House of Commons.	☐	☐
(d) Every word said in the House of Commons and the Lords is written down in a book for anyone to read.	☐	☐
(e) MPs are elected for life.	☐	☐
(f) There is not enough room for all the MPs to fit in the House of Commons chamber.	☐	☐
(g) The bar of the House is where MPs get drunk.	☐	☐
(h) The Strangers' Gallery is for MPs who are strange.	☐	☐
(i) Laws have to pass between both Houses of Parliament so there is time to consider them in detail.	☐	☐
(j) The House of Commons gets most of its debating done in the morning.	☐	☐

3 Make any changes you need to write down 10 correct statements about Parliament.

Democracy and Parliament

> 'Politics is rarely admired as a profession and perhaps this is as it should be. We direct the lives of fellow citizens, tax their incomes and, in the end, are doomed to disappoint their expectations.'
> John Major, *Autobiography* (Harper Collins, 2000)

Wanted – an elected representative of the people of Great Britain

Salary c.£50,000 (rising to over £100,000 with promotion) plus expenses of up to £50,000

Job Description

Must be over 21 years of age
Should be prepared to be in opposition for years
Renewable contract every 5 years, or less if election called
Work late into the night
Be available to vote in debates called at any time
Work in central London, but with long holidays
Travel regularly between **Westminster** and your **constituency**
Be familiar with any subject the government passes laws on
Make yourself available to talk to your constituents regularly
Stick to the promises made in your party's **manifesto**
Look after the interests of up to 100,000 people in your constituency
Be prepared to run any government department if invited
Answer hundreds of letters and respond to requests for interviews and meetings
Respond to pressure put on you to vote how your party wants
Have a role to play in making laws and changing the country
Ask questions of the government to check on them

TASK

Would you like to be an MP? Read the think bubbles and job description and separate out the pros and cons. Add any of your own that you can think of.

Elections: choosing the right person for the job

At least once every five years, there is a general election when all the MPs in the House of Commons have to go back to their constituencies and ask to be re-elected. If they have done a bad job, or their Party has become unpopular, they can be removed from power. This means that at the end of the election every area should have an MP who has more support than any one else in their area.

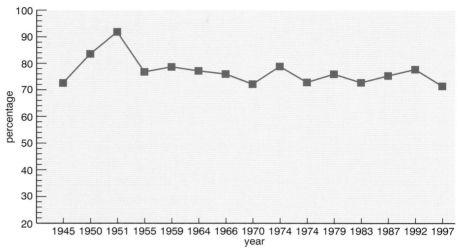

▲ General Election turnout

Large numbers of people do not vote and this means they are not playing a part in choosing their local MP. Some people think this reflects the way we are expected to vote. They say that in countries where voting is made easier, for example, where people can vote by post, the figures go up. Others argue that people do not vote because they are bored by all politicians and believe that whoever wins the election, they will be pretty much the same as everyone else in government.

This can have a big effect on how representative the government is. In 1997, the Labour government came to power with 419 MPs out of a total of 659, that is 64% of all MPs. Only 71% of all the people who could vote, bothered, and only 43% of those voted Labour. This means 31% of all the adults in the country voted Labour or, to look at it another way, 7 people in every 10 did not vote for Labour.

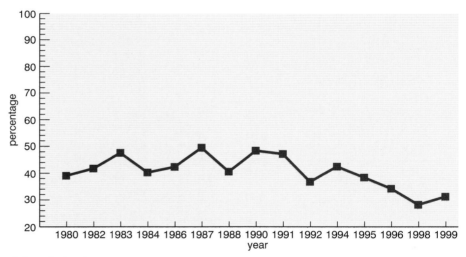

▲ Local election turnout

TASKS

1 Why do you think there is such a difference between local and national election turnout?

2 Do you think it matters if people do not vote?

3 What could politicians do to encourage more people to vote?

4 Some countries have compulsory voting. This means that if you do not vote you can be fined. Do you think this is a good idea? Discuss it as a class and come up with suggestions.

The work of charities

Charities are a very important part of the world we live in. There are thousands of charities in the UK. They do not exist to make profits, but are based instead on meeting a social need.

Look through the following examples of people meeting a social need and explain whether each one is an example of an act of charity. Give reasons for your answers.

SKILLS FOCUS

- Thinking about people's motives and a variety of points of view

Example 1

Maxine works in a hospital. She is a nurse and spends most of her time looking after people who are ill with very serious diseases. She spends as much of her time as possible talking to the patients and trying to comfort them. She also tries to make time for people who come to visit their friends and relatives, as they often get upset.

Example 2

Jim visits the local hospital two evenings per week. He is the local vicar and spends this time visiting people who are sick but have no friends or relatives to come and see them. Sometimes Jim is the only person to visit them from one week to the next.

Example 3

Margaret plays the tambourine with the local Salvation Army band. Every holiday they go along to the local hospital to play music to entertain and cheer up the patients. The whole band gives up their time for free and also practises regularly through the week.

Example 4

Henry volunteers as a buddy for the Terence Higgins Trust. He visits Mike, who is ill with AIDS, once a week at home or hospital. Henry went on a training course to learn important skills to help Mike.

TASKS

What does charity mean to you?

1 These examples all show people doing good deeds. Are they all acts of charity?

2 What makes some actions 'charitable' and others just good?

3 Look at the following definitions taken from different dictionaries. Choose a definition that you think best describes what a charity is. If you do not agree with any of them, make up your own and write it in your notes.

Charity means:

'an institution for the benefit of others'

'feelings or acts of affection'

'government provision for the relief of the poor'

'universal love'

'being devoted to caring for those in need of help'

'thinking favourably of others and doing good'

'something that is given up to help the needy'.

USEFUL WORDS

Volunteer – someone who gives up his or her time without payment

Donation – gift of money or something else to a charity

Compassion – helping people because of feelings of sympathy

Charity in the not-so-distant past

Since 1945, the UK has developed a Welfare State in which people are able to claim benefits, medical treatment and other services as a right. Before that time, many of these were seen as charity and were organised by individuals – they decided who should and should not receive help and on what terms.

'Charity begins at home, but should not end there.'
Thomas Fuller, 1732

'Mrs Jellyby,' said Mr Kenge, standing with his back to the fire, and casting his eyes over the dusty hearth-rug as if it were Mrs Jellyby's biography, 'is a lady of very remarkable strength of character, who devotes herself entirely to the public. She has devoted herself to an **extensive** variety of public subjects, at various times, and is at present (until something else attracts her) devoted to the subject of Africa.'

... We passed several more children on the way up, whom it was difficult to avoid treading on in the dark; and as we came into Mrs Jellyby's presence, one of the poor little things fell down-stairs – down a whole flight (as it sounded to me), with a great noise.

Mrs Jellyby, whose face reflected none of the **uneasiness** which we could not help showing in our own faces as the dear child's head recorded its passage with a bump on every stair – Richard afterwards said he counted seven, besides one for the landing – received us with perfect **equanimity**. She was a pretty, very **diminutive**, plump woman, of from forty to fifty, with handsome eyes, though they had a curious habit of seeming to look a long way off. As if – I am quoting Richard again – they could see nothing nearer than Africa!

... 'You find me, my dears,' said Mrs Jellyby, 'You find me, my dears, as usual, very busy; but that you will excuse. The African project at present employs my whole time. It involves me in correspondence with public bodies, and with private individuals anxious for the welfare of their **species** all over the country.'

From Charles Dickens, *Bleak House*, Chapter 4 (1853)

GLOSSARY

Extensive – very big

Uneasiness – worry

Equanimity – calm

Diminutive – small

Species – people

TASKS

1 Who is Mrs Jellyby concerned for?

2 What does she do when the child falls down the stairs?

3 Why do you think she responds in this way?

4 What do you think the author thinks of people like Mrs Jellyby?

5 What do you think of Mrs Jellyby?

6 Why might people like Mrs Jellyby take up charitable work?

November, 1932   sunset 4:30pm

I do not know how much more help I can give the poor of this Parish. The Depression is hitting us all so hard. My allowance of five shillings a month cannot stretch to everybody I need to support. It breaks my heart when I have to turn people away from the door as I have no more shillings to give away. Their gaunt, grey faces stay with me into my nightmares.

At least my wife and I can go on collecting unwanted and outgrown clothes from my parishioners. They have been kind. I cannot collect enough shoes and boots, they are more valuable than any riches a man could have in these cruel times. The relief on that fellow's face the other night was a brief glimmer of the good we can all do. I had no money left but as I looked at his ragged clothes, I could give him one of my overcoats and an almost decent pair of boots. Small comfort against those bitter winter nights. If only I could do more ...

From the Reverend Samuel Rodelly's diary

TASKS

1 Why is Samuel Rodelly upset?

2 What makes him happy?

3 Why does he do this? Think about what need there is and what Samuel gets out of it.

When you have read both the extracts, discuss the following:

'What are the advantages and disadvantages of leaving charity to the goodwill of individuals?'

Helping others

Why do people give to charity and what are the personal and social results that these actions can have?

TASKS

1 What is the message of the cartoon strip?

2 List the ways in which the public help charities. Use the cartoon strip to help you and add any other ones you know. Try and draw an extra frame for the strip.

Often, by helping others we help ourselves. This is especially true when applied to charity work, whether it involves being a **volunteer** or giving. The problems illustrated by the photos are dealt with by charities using **donations** given by the public.

▲ Friends of the Earth

▲ Barnardo's

ACTIVITY

Discuss in groups all the actions currently undertaken by charities and make notes on them. Then discuss the consequences for future society, ie for YOU, if there were no groups or individuals ready to help tackle the problems you see given here. Think about disease, crime, pollution, danger, etc. You could either write down the discussion you have or draw your own picture to illustrate how things would change.

Using the help on offer

'The only gift is a portion of thyself.'
The American essayist, Ralph Emerson, in 1844

There are about 500,000 voluntary organisations in existence in Britain and around 170,000 of them are official charities. Their work covers a vast area and the problems they help with are hugely varied. They range from large organisations that deal with high-profile issues, such as drug abuse, to small groups that give advice to sufferers from very rare diseases. Finding the organisation that can help may be time-consuming but worthwhile in the end. And if it does not yet exist, you can start it!

Who can I turn to?

(a) My neighbour is very elderly and is not coping. She wants to remain independent but she cannot carry her own shopping and I worry she is not eating.

(b) My brother left home six months ago. He just upped and went, didn't say a word and since then, we've heard nothing from him. He's a grown-up and can do what he likes but we'd like to know he's OK.

(c) There are people in my street who keep a big dog. I see the poor thing chained up in the garden. You can't get too near it because of the stink! That poor animal never moves from there and no one clears up after him.

(d) I am fed up! I've written to everyone I can think of but no one seems prepared to DO anything. My kids play near a stream at the back of our house and the water is bright pink! It can't be healthy, can it? I blame the factory.

(e) My heart was in my mouth! I was running across the street when I heard this baby sort of gurgling. I looked up and saw this tiny child on the window sill, three storeys up and trying to wave to me! I was terrified and very angry. What was the baby's window doing open at 7:30 in the morning on a cold, wet December day? I know the mother, saw her beat the older child once.

(f) It's my grandfather. You know he was terribly wounded in the last war? Well, up to now, he's been able to manage but these last few months, he has got worse. He's almost blind now and very feeble but he hates to ask for help. The idea of going into a Home for the Elderly fills him with dread.

TASKS

1 Which charity should each speaker apply to for advice or help?

2 Are there any other local groups you know about who could help the people in these examples?

3 Find out more about the work of one of these charities and make a presentation about it to the class. Alternatively, as a class, put together a display showing the work of local charities.

4 Find out how you or your school could help each of these charities.

The UK's leading charity specialising in child protection and the prevention of cruelty to children.

Dedicated to the care of people affected by cancer and the enhancement of their quality of life.

Friends of the Earth

Committed to the conservation, protection and improvement of the environment.

The relief of poverty, sickness, suffering, disease, incapacity or old age and re-establishing links with missing persons.

Safeguards the welfare, interests and memory of those who have served in the armed forces, and their dependants.

A free National Helpline for children in trouble or danger.

Provides practical support and advice to assist older people to live independent lives.

Shelter

The relief of hardship and distress amongst homeless people.

Compassion fatigue?

'*The more I give, the more they want. I donate money on a regular basis, I do voluntary work and I am very happy about doing both. But I get a letter almost every day from some charity or other, asking for more and suggesting how much I should give. It makes me furious! How can the charities justify this use of money; they waste it on free pencils, shiny photographs and endless mail-shots. I object to the emotional blackmail they are using too.*'
B.E.Bryan

'*I think it's a good thing that charities are finally experimenting with new ways to encourage people to give money. The other day I had an envelope with 10 pence stuck in it and the letter said please send this back, with some extra money added. It was very clever and I felt really guilty until I sent it back, I didn't want to feel that I had kept their 10 pence. If it works I think that is all that really matters.*'
S.W.Price

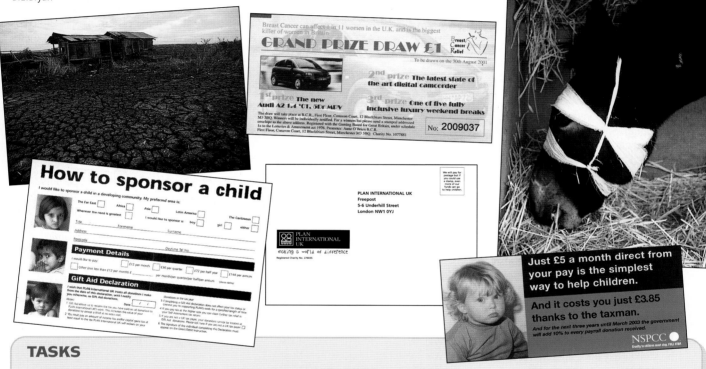

TASKS

1 How do you feel about each of the techniques and images outlined above?

2 How are we being persuaded to send money? Clearly explain the tactics used for each of the letters and photos.

3 What do you think about the two opinions at the top of this page? Give reasons for your views.

'**Compassion** fatigue' is the term used when people have grown tired of being asked to volunteer, to give money or to worry about the problems of others. Some people argue that there is a limit to the number of people and situations one can feel bad about and that, eventually, people ignore appeals for help and say they have to think about themselves.

TASKS

1 What do some people think causes 'compassion fatigue'?

2 Would you have any sympathy for those who feel they do not want to help any longer?

3 Some people spend their whole lives helping others. Why don't they suffer from 'compassion fatigue'?

Fundraising and volunteering

It is often the same people who volunteer to help every time. Why do they do it? Where would we be without these volunteers? Perhaps this section will set you thinking about how YOU might get involved in voluntary activities, possibly school-based at first, but your experience there can be carried over into public activities too.

Nightmare on Elm Avenue

Elm Avenue Junior School held its annual School Fayre last Saturday with the aim of raising money to buy sports equipment. With luck, the school will be able to purchase two or three tennis balls at most after that "fund-raising" event.

Why did the organisers imagine there would be fine weather and, as I was told, not bother to insure the event against rain? When I arrived, the school playground was a multicoloured sea of mud, rain and tissue paper. I was wet, as there was nowhere to park my car near by, and I joined a small queue of parents who had been let into the secret of the Fayre's opening time: it certainly was not on the few posters I saw.

Inside the small school hall was a scene of utter chaos. Children ran around screaming, trying to set up what was left of their stalls in the little space available. It was my intention to get something to eat and drink while I waited for the Fayre to get under way but there was not enough food even for these small numbers. The stalls and games were very familiar, the same as last year and the year before, and the prizes were not of the kind to encourage one to spend money on a boring game.

Conflict and work

▼ Child **labour**

It has been estimated that nearly 2 million children work in Britain. These young people are often employed illegally, or in dangerous situations, and sometimes work for as little as 50p per hour.

Wanting to stand on your own two feet, earn a little extra pocket money and learn about the world of work are worthwhile goals. However, this can often cause **conflict** at home or at school. You may think wanting to work has nothing to do with your parents/carers or school – it is your life. Is it though? ... are you fully aware of the laws regarding legal work at the age of 13?

SKILLS FOCUS

- Discussion skills
- Finding solutions

USEFUL WORDS

Labour – work

Conflict – disagreement between different interests

Confrontation – a situation in which people deal with differences of opinion face to face

Strike – workers refuse to work in order to put pressure on employers to accept their demands

Redundancies – this refers to workers being laid off when their job is no longer required by the employer. This is different from being 'sacked', which is linked to poor performance in a job.

TASKS

1 Look at the advertisements on this page. Which would you be interested in?

2 What protests or objections might come from a) home b) school?

3 How might you persuade parents/carers or teachers that a part-time job would be a good idea?

4 Look at the fact box and think about which of the jobs advertised would be legal for you. You may have to check with your local council for local regulations.

FACTS

Under 13 years – only certain occasional work allowed, such as helping neighbours, etc.

13–15 years – you cannot work before 7am or after 7pm. You cannot be employed to work during school hours. You cannot work more than 2 hours on a school day or a Sunday.

16 years – varies for local areas.

Join our gang! Deliver the local newspaper once a week come rain or shine. If you are aged between 13 and 65 don't hesitate, phone immediately on 020 8123 4567

Boy/girl WANTED for local fish and chip shop at weekends, 11:30am–8:30pm. Good rates of pay offered. No experience needed. Apply in writing to Mr A H Addock, A Plaice Beyond, 2 High Street, Seatown.

HELP! Babysitter required 3 nights per week. Mon, Wed and Thursday, 6-10pm. Desperate mum will pay top rates. Phone after 5pm any night. Mrs I Gotcha 7796 342 1734

SATURDAY GIRL/BOY NEEDED. Busy market stall looking for someone who is not afraid of hard work and the cold! WE WILL TEACH YOU TO SELL IF YOU CAN YELL. 10am-3pm. Pop down and talk to me, Mark Ett-Stall, 37 The Broadwalk.

LOCAL HAIRDRESSER ✂ – Keen young junior wanted. Do you like people? Do you like chatting and gossiping? Then you could be just who we are looking for, £3.00 an hour – 5 hours every Sunday. Contact Sally Snippen, The Cut Off, High Street.

Problems at work!

Brooke, aged 14, has succeeded in getting a Saturday job that she hopes will also mean a holiday job and a steady supply of money that will enable her to buy some of the shoes she will be selling. How easy will it be for her to make the transition from school rules to work rules?

TASKS

1 Working in groups, discuss what expectations of work you think Brooke had.

2 Both Brooke and the supervisor made mistakes. What were they?

3 Working in pairs, take one scene and act it out:

(a) as it's shown

(b) in a less confrontational way.

4 Have people in your class had, or heard of, problems at work? How did they work them out?

The trade unions

This section is about the history of trade unions, what they were originally set up to do and their role in society today.

More people in Britain have union membership cards than credit cards! Union members may be university lecturers and doctors or they may be street-cleaners or cooks. Relatively little news of the trade union movement is currently given by the media, especially if compared with the 1970s, when the unions were powerful enough to call a series of **strikes** and even to bring down a government. Since then laws like the 1980 Employment Act have been effective in cutting the power of the unions.

The word 'union' appeared only in 1900 but groups of workers combined to protect their common interests as early as the Middle Ages, when the guilds were formed. Over time many were arrested and punished for their efforts. In 1824, however, the law forbidding 'combinations' was cancelled and in 1871, unions were granted the right to strike. This right was exercised in 1926 when industry came to a stop during the General Strike, after the government allowed employers to cut the wages of the miners who, at the time, were a large and powerful workforce.

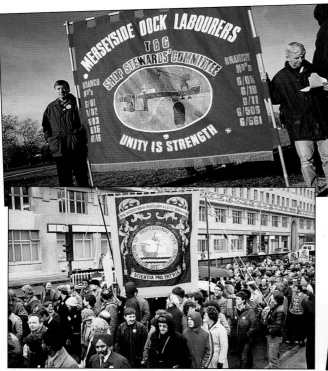

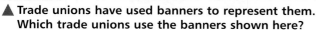

▲ Trade unions have used banners to represent them. Which trade unions use the banners shown here?

TASKS

1 Explain in your own words why trade unions were formed.

2 Why do people join trade unions? What are the benefits of membership for individuals?

3 What are the benefits for employers?

4 Are there any drawbacks to having trade unions?

5 Find out how many of the people you know belong to unions and list the names of the unions. Ask those people WHY they are members.

The trade union movement

There are people who believe that the trade unions in Britain belong to history and are of no use today. These people believe that circumstances have changed and that a new type of organisation is needed to deal with the new situation – for example, to negotiate with the powerful multinational corporations that control industry in Britain, as in many other parts of the world. Instead, the unions remain locked in the past, fighting a class war and looking after the welfare of a group of workers in one skill-area only. This page will look at some of the arguments for and against the trade unions.

A TRADE UNION

- protects and improves working conditions
- works for better pay, shorter working hours
- tries to prevent **redundancies** and unemployment
- provides training
- ensures safety at work
- ensures all workers have equal rights
- helps and advises in time of conflict with an employer

A balanced argument?

(a) A union can help in situations where the individual would be powerless.

(b) The union has the power to negotiate and get better pay.

(c) The union can protect the rights of workers at all levels.

(d) The union can bring about social change.

(e) Unions represent the workers as officers are democratically elected.

(f) The unions are beginning to merge and form larger groups with more bargaining power.

On the other hand ...

However, ...

Nevertheless, ...

A counter argument would be ...

Looking at it from another angle, ...

It could equally well be said that ...

(1) Unions tend to make unrealistically high claims and so lose public sympathy.

(2) Unions are interested in making sure there are differences in pay to reflect different levels of skill.

(3) The pay and conditions of union officers means they are out of touch with the grassroots workers.

(4) There is still rivalry between the unions.

(5) Unions have a tendency to concentrate on short-term money-based issues.

(6) Unions are prepared to help only those who are members and who agree fully with the union's policies.

TASKS

1 Use the sentences in the second box to find counter arguments to those in the first box. Begin your counter arguments with the linking words in the middle.

2 Write a balanced argument about the role of the unions.

3 Do any of the working adults you know belong to a trade union? If so, why?

4 Do you think you would join a trade union when you start work? Explain your reasons.

5 If you have an idea about what job you would like to do when you are older, try to find out which union would be relevant to you.

Consumer rights

When you buy goods or services you are entering into a contract with the seller even though nothing has been written down. This contract gives you both certain rights and responsibilities.

Shopping: a cause of conflict

Shopping has become a major leisure pursuit and it is very easy to get carried away by the wide choice available or by the tempting 'special offers' and end up, at home, with unsuitable and unwanted goods. What can you do?

Some stores allow you to exchange your goods, provided they are in perfect condition and you take them back very quickly. But in law, you have no rights if you have simply changed your mind about the purchase. Also, there is nothing you can do if you have damaged the item or used it and then decide that you no longer want it, or if it was sold as damaged. Shoppers have rights: all goods sold must be of satisfactory quality, do what is expected of them and meet the description on the packaging or the display sign.

How to complain

Let the shop know as soon as possible that you are not satisfied, by telephone if that is quicker, and then return the item to the shop, with the receipt or guarantee. Losing the receipt does not deprive you of your rights but it does help prove where and when you bought the item. If the item is bulky or heavy, it is the responsibility of the shopkeeper to collect it.

You can also tell the shopkeeper or manager what you want: a credit note, repairs, replacement or your money back. This applies to sale goods too. Notices saying that there are no refunds on sale goods are not legal.

If there is still a problem, a letter should be written. That letter should:
- Describe the item
- Say when and where you bought it and give the price
- Explain what is wrong
- Say what you have already done
- Say what you want
- Use recorded delivery to post the letter
- Send copies of receipts, etc, keeping the originals yourself
- Keep a copy of your letter

ACTIVITY – ROLE PLAY

1 Choose an item you want to return to the shop. It could be one of the items shown on this page, or a real item that was unsatisfactory. Decide what the problem is and think about your legal rights described on this page.

2 Work with a partner and act out a scene between a shop manager and a dissatisfied customer. It can take place in the shop or on the telephone. Explain what preparations you will make before speaking.

3 Show your role play to others in the class and ask for their tips about how to improve it so the customer receives the best solution for them.

4 If you do not feel you have had your rights taken seriously in a shop you can take your complaint further, to senior managers. Write a letter of complaint following up one of the unsuccessful role plays. Give all the details needed and say who you have already spoken to on the phone or in the shop and what happened. Make a convincing argument to get what you want.

The Small Claims Court

If you cannot agree a solution in conflicts over your legal rights, you can take your case to court. This is often a slow, complicated and very expensive business but there is a simpler and cheaper option open to British citizens. It is the Small Claims Court and you will learn about it in this section.

The Small Claims track

When every other method has failed, you can go to court to sue for compensation or to claim your money back. The County Court handles these issues, which usually involve consumer claims like those already mentioned, as well as accidents, disputes about repairs between landlords and tenants, rent arrears and actions up to the sum of £5,000* (£1,000 in N. Ireland and £750 in Scotland).

The atmosphere in the Small Claims Court is informal and there is no need for a solicitor to argue the case. The language used is simple and, without lawyers, the cost of the case is not so expensive as it would be otherwise. There

are usually no difficult points of law in these actions and no one can offer expert evidence without the judge's permission. Few or no witnesses are called, but the person who brings the case, the Claimant, can ask another person to speak for him or her if that is preferred.

The cases are heard in public but the claimant and the defendant are

expected to accept the judge's decision. An appeal can only be lodged if the procedure was faulty and then the case may go to a higher court with the delay and expense that would then follow.

* In certain circumstances, larger sums may be claimed but the issues must be simple in legal terms AND both claimant and defendant must agree on the sum.

TASKS

1 List the advantages of using a Small Claims Court instead of a Higher Court.

2 Work in groups and choose a judge, claimant and a defendant. Act out a case. This could be based on one of the unresolved conflicts from page 46.

3 Does everyone agree with the judge's decision? Can you come to a whole class agreement about a fair decision in this case?

Who can help?

Trading Standards Service
www.tradingstandards.gov.uk
Check prices, weights and measures and the safety of goods.

Citizens Advice Bureaux
www.nacab.org.uk
Give advice on consumer issues and help with form-filling and advise on a vast range of problems.

Community Legal Service
www.justask.org.uk
Give advice and information on the rights of every citizen.

REMEMBER! The organisations listed above are there to help you. Use them!

ACTIVITY: REVIEWING THE CHAPTER

This chapter has been looking at conflicts that can arise because of our role in the economy. Whether you are a worker or a customer, you may still have to stand up for your rights. You also have to think about how you can solve disagreements so that the outcome is fair. At the end of

the day, even if your rights are being denied in some ways, most people would not have full arguments about them the whole time. They would try to find different ways to solve the difficulties.

Look through all the problems in this chapter and try to draw up some guidelines for workers or

customers. Think about their legal rights, who can help, and ways to manage a conflict so that it does not get out of hand.

Once the guidelines are ready you could try to role play some of the situations in the chapter to see if following the advice makes the outcome any better.

Media power?

People in the UK spend almost 16 hours per week listening to the radio. More daily national and regional newspapers are sold for every person in Britain than in most other developed countries. There are an estimated 5 million Internet users in Britain and most teenagers claim they could not live if they did not have TV. In one survey 21% of people said they watched 36 hours of TV every week.

There are five free-to-air television channels in Britain. BBC1 and BBC2 are publicly funded – your parents or carers pay for these channels when the licence is due. There are also satellite and cable channels paid for by subscription. The largest satellite programme is BSkyB, which has over 5 million subscribers and dominates paid-for television in Britain.

We are surrounded by groups of talented, rich, creative people who are working long hours and spending vast amounts of money in an attempt to persuade us to buy their product, to shop at their store, to go where they want us to go and to do what they want us to do.

Do we understand what they are doing? Can we resist the temptations they offer? Does it matter?

Brief description of the advertisement	My first response is ...	The aim of the advertiser is ...	Success rate out of 10 ..
1			
2			
3			

A Good Print Advertisement

... makes an impact

...presents an image that arouses your curiosity

...uses photographs

...uses well-known people

...focuses on one person, not a group

...chooses a modern scene: history is considered boring

...presents ONE, big memorable idea

...has a memorable slogan

...fixes the brand name in your mind. This is most important

From *Ogilvy on Advertising* by David Ogilvy

Alex Upton | AGE 29

TASKS

1 What are your first impressions of each of these adverts? How do they make you feel?

2 What do you think the aims of the advertiser are? What might they want to achieve through this advert?

3 On a scale of 1 to 10, with 10 being very successful, what rating would you give each advert in achieving its aims?

4 What are the main differences between these two adverts?

Collect some more examples of adverts from newspapers and magazines before completing the next task.

5 Experts in the creation of successful print advertising have tried to give others a 'recipe for success'. Some of their suggestions appear in the box in the centre of the page. Do each of the adverts meet all, some or none of those criteria? Use your findings to complete the chart.

6 Imagine that one of the advertisers on this page is going to commission a new follow up set campaign. They want to build on the success of their previous adverts and maintain the interests of their target audience. You should prepare an outline for an advertising campaign. In your presentation you should have some drawings and ideas for a caption to illustrate what the advert might look like. But you should also include the following information:

• What is the aim of your advert?

• What message do you want to get across?

• What action do you hope people will take because of the advert?

• Who are you aiming at?

• How does your advert idea connect with your target audience?

• Are you likely to offend anyone with your advert?

• Why do you think this advert will work?

Once the work is completed, present your ideas to others in the class. Ask them to rate the advertising idea. Once the best has been selected, consider it as a class.

• What makes the advert a good one?

• Would it affect people in your class?

Between the lines – reading teenagers' magazines then and now

A visit to a newsagent's proves that there are now magazines for all ages and to satisfy all interests. Teenagers' magazines occupy a large part of the market.

Forty or fifty years ago the ideal teenager in magazines was often excellent at sport and was deeply proud of and loyal to the school she or he attended. Although living in a sheltered world, usually far from the city, these young people had exciting adventures; they unmasked spies, released hostages and foiled burglaries.

Now, magazines aimed at young people are very different. They often show more realistic stories; they try to engage more with the real issues they think young people are facing.

TASK

Look at the magazines reproduced below and describe the differences between them. List the strengths and weaknesses of the old and modern magazines respectively. What does this tell you

(a) about the ways in which young people's lives have changed and

(b) about the changing expectations of young people?

The power of advertising

Advertisers are targeting teenagers for every passing trend. Allowances and pocket money may not stretch to pay for the latest crazes or designer gear but wearing down parents' and carers' resistance may empty their purses or wallets instead.

Millions of pounds every year are spent by manufacturers on promoting their products. Large companies publicise their goods to encourage you to buy their products rather than any other brand. They also want to create a demand for items which are not really necessary. Brand names, logos and jingles are all used by advertisers to draw you into buying products whether you need them or not.

ACTIVITY

The power of advertising

Collect as many advertisements as you can from the magazines you read. Work with a partner (or on your own) and categorise your advertisements in the following way:

From the experience of this exercise did you discover that most advertisements were aimed at girls, boys or both sexes?

Were results different for different types of magazine?

What conclusions can you draw from your research?

Advertising makes us want to own the best, the biggest, the flashiest, the trendiest-named object. Can you think of any other influences that put pressure on you to buy brands? Which are the most important influences on you?

Magazine	Product	Prices (if shown)	Age group	Aimed at girls, boys or both

Soap operas: have they a role to play in society?

Over 98% of the population of Great Britain own a TV set. Many of those viewers will be following the adventures shown in one or more of the soap operas. In this section you will be considering the role of the 'soaps' and deciding whether they have a positive or a negative influence on viewers.

You will have your own opinion on the value or otherwise of watching soap operas on a regular basis. Many people today believe that soaps fulfil a useful function and that they are no more and no less than a modern type of storytelling.

They offer a wide range of interesting experiences including those which are 'taboo', eg euthanasia

They offer companionship; lonely people get to know a group of people and can share their lives

They present us with the sort of problems that we encounter in life

They provide a topic of conversation for the playground and workplace

They show ways of behaving in many situations, ways that we may one day find useful

They present us with a range of role models and teach us to judge character in others and in ourselves

They offer a way of escape from boring reality, as books and films do.

They teach indirectly and pass on important information about the society we live in

They keep young people at home, out of trouble, and sharing something with the family

TASKS

In the diamond are some of the reasons why soap operas may have a positive influence on viewers.

1 Working in groups, diamond-rank them – ie, arrange them in a diamond-shaped pattern, with the most important at the top, and the least important at the bottom.

2 Compare your group's ranking with the those of the other groups.

3 List any other arguments you can think of to support soap operas.

1 Britt Street
Angleton
GB3 6BG

The Editor
The British Courier
Press Street
London E46 2SA

3rd August 2000

Dear Sir,

I call upon the parents of Great Britain to join me in forming a new pressure group that will bring great benefit to our children, and, in the long term, to society as a whole.

The aims of this group, which I propose to call APAT (Association of Parents for the Abolition of Television) include the removal of TV sets from all homes, schools and buildings where they may be seen by persons under the age of 18 years.

My own experience – I am the father of four children aged between 9 and 16 – has convinced me of the terrible effect of the medium on young people. The greatest problem is caused by the soaps, those unoriginal attempts at story-telling that appear to take up to two thirds of the viewing time.

They are unrealistic, full of violent, foul-mouthed people who lead lives so full of drama and event that a normal person would be dead from stress after just one episode. Perhaps that is why they have no energy for the tedious part of life like work. I doubt whether young people are capable of distinguishing between reality and fantasy. Certainly my children discuss these characters as if they were real people. The role models provided by these soaps persuade the young to drink, smoke, be violent and to tell lies. Furthermore, the young see their own lives as dull and uneventful if they are not in love or in a state of conflict with all those around them.

Young people no longer communicate with their parents. They prefer to slump on the sofa and sit there, passively absorbing the idea that life's problems can be solved by actions whose consequences are rarely or ever shown.

There is no need to say that my children now never pick up a book and have to stay up very late in order to complete a pathetically small amount of homework.

I ask all responsible parents and teachers to join APAT and help eradicate this evil force in our midst.

Yours faithfully,

Septimus Grows

TASKS

1 Write a letter to the same newspaper and answer his criticisms, point by point, proving that soap operas play a very positive role in the life of the nation.

2 Have a classroom debate about whether soap operas are good or bad. Think about the different points of view that have been expressed. What do you really think?

You could debate the following quote:

'The reason why soaps are so popular is because they're a relief from the tedium of your own life'

(From 'Soaplife' by Jemma Walker, in *Family Affairs*, December 2000)

Use the list of typical soap issues below to help you.

Abortion	Gossip
Blackmail	Anguish
Divorce	Teenage torment
Disagreements	Heartache
Car crashes	Prison
Abduction	Betrayal
Wickedness	Loneliness
Danger	Punch-ups
Robbery	Deceit
Court cases	Arguments
Babies	Theft
Suicide	Bigamy
Murder	Custody
Drug abuse	Love
Bodies	Lies
Nightmare	Adoption
Bullying	

Britain and the wider world

Britain and the European Union

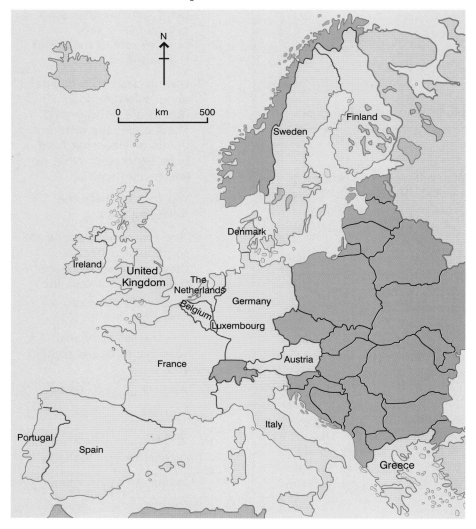

USEFUL WORDS

Treaty – an agreement between countries

Colony – an area or country which is controlled by another country: eg, India was a colony of Britain

Imperial – anything which is part of an 'empire', ie a collection of countries ruled by one

Civil service – the part of government that carries out the administration, ie planning, monitoring, reporting, etc.

Consensus – agreement

Charter – written description of what an organisation is for and how it will work

United Nations Declaration of Human Rights – the list of individual rights that the United Nations tries to protect

History of the European Union

After World War 2, European countries were keen to cooperate with each other. They wanted to make sure that another European war could never happen again by joining together to form the European Union (EU).

1952	The European Iron and Steel Community Treaty was signed by France, Germany, Italy, the Netherlands, Belgium and Luxembourg.
1957	The European Atomic Energy Community (Euratom) extended cooperation to nuclear fuel.
	The European Economic Community (EEC) created a 'common market'. Member states increased cooperation on foreign trade and agriculture.
1973	Denmark, Ireland and the UK joined the EEC.
1981	Greece joined the EEC.
1986	Spain and Portugal joined the EEC.
	A 'single market' was created. This meant that goods, services, people and capital (money) could move freely between all 12 EEC countries.
1992	The Maastricht Treaty created the European Union. Cooperation was extended to include foreign affairs and justice.
1995	Austria, Finland and Sweden joined the EU.
1997	The Amsterdam Treaty was agreed to prepare the EU to accept more members in the future.

How the EU works

1 The Council of the EU

The Council is the main decision-making body. It is made up of representatives from the governments of all the EU member countries. Important meetings are attended by all 15 of the prime ministers and presidents. However, other meetings are attended by the relevant minister: for example, if the Council is discussing farming, it will be attended by the 15 ministers responsible for agriculture.

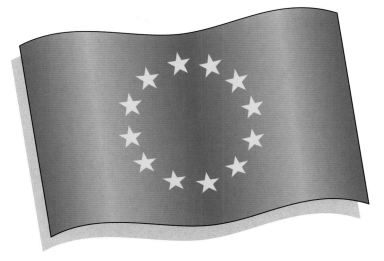

3 The European Parliament

The Parliament was originally just asked for its opinions on laws but recently its duties have widened. Now it has joint power to pass laws with the Council of the EU in areas such as education, the single market and the environment. It is made up of 626 Members of the European Parliament (MEPs), who are elected by voters in each member country.

2 The European Commission

The Commission puts ideas forward to the Council and the European Parliament. It also makes sure laws are carried out once they have been passed. Each country in the EU chooses one or two members to join the Commission. These appointments must be agreed by the Parliament and last for five years. Each Commissioner has an area of responsibility, such as Trade, Environment, Transport, etc.

The EU distributes money to poorer areas in member states to help them provide jobs

The EU gives money and advice to help poorer countries all over the world

There are 11 official languages in the EU. The Commission employs about 8,000 translators to help people work together

The EU sets quotas for fish catches to try to preserve fish populations

The EU Commission can take member states to court for breaking EU rules and laws

The number of votes each country has in the Council of the EU depends on the size of each country: eg, Germany, France, Italy and the UK have 10 votes each, but Luxembourg only has 2

Some people argue the EU should become a single super-state, to make it easier to compete with the USA

The EU is developing cooperation for defence and peace-keeping

TASKS

1 Look at the map. Which countries do you think would be most likely to join the EU next?

2 Why do you think the first treaty of the EU was about coal and steel?

3 Make a list of the other activities that the EU undertakes.

4 What are the advantages of working together on these issues?

5 Are there any issues you think the EU should not be involved with?

6 In 1997 just over 70% of those who were eligible voted in the General Election in the UK. In 1999 less than a third voted in the European election. Why do you think people in the UK are less likely to vote in European elections?

Britain and the Commonwealth

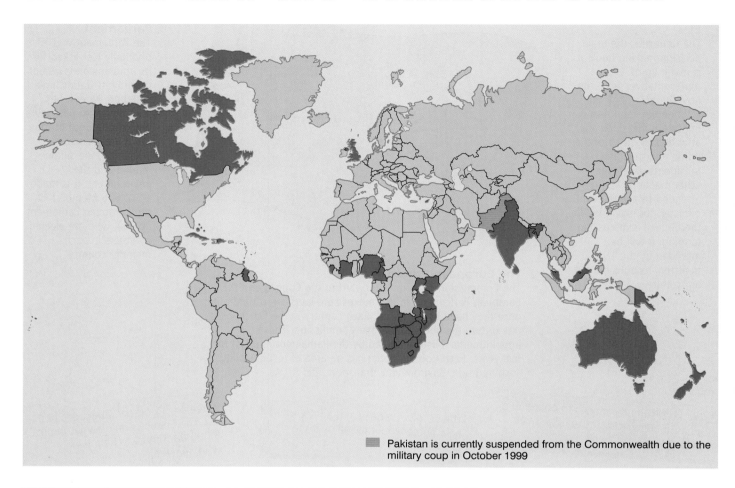

Pakistan is currently suspended from the Commonwealth due to the military coup in October 1999

History of the Commonwealth

1867 Canada was the first **colony** to become a 'dominion', ie self-governing with equal status to the UK.

1926 **Imperial** Conference held, at which the Balfour Report, defining the British Commonwealth of Nations, was agreed.

1930 First Commonwealth Games held (called the Empire Games at the time).

1931 The British Commonwealth of Nations definition was adopted into British law.

1949 The word 'British' was dropped from the Commonwealth. India became the first member not to have the Queen as Head of State.

1965 The Commonwealth Secretariat, the Commonwealth's **civil service**, was established.

1971 Singapore Declaration of Commonwealth Principles.

1991 Harare Declaration confirmed the principles of the Commonwealth and allowed Mozambique to join as the only member that had not been a part of the British Empire.

Structure of the Commonwealth

How do people join?
To join the Commonwealth, a country:
- should be a sovereign nation
- should have been linked with an existing Commonwealth member
- must agree with Commonwealth values, principles and priorities as set out in the Harare Declaration.

Who is the head?
HM Queen Elizabeth II is the Head of the Commonwealth.

How does it make decisions?
The Commonwealth Heads of Government have meetings (CHOGMs) every two years. Requests for help (for example on managing elections, or trade advice) are made by member governments. Decisions are in line with the Harare Declaration.

How does it implement decisions?
The Commonwealth Secretariat puts decisions into practice. High-level assistance is provided by government ministers.

Mozambique was granted membership for its stand against minority white rule, whilst South Africa's membership was withdrawn between 1961 and 1994 because of its apartheid regime

The Commonwealth Foundation was established in 1996 to support the non-governmental sectors of the Commonwealth with financial and other assistance

'The Commonwealth still exists because its members have decided for themselves that these values are worth cherishing'. HM The Prince of Wales, February 2000

'One of the reasons many countries support the Commonwealth is because they can have their views magnified through joining with others and hence see the value of playing a part in local, regional and global **consensus**-building'. Don McKinnon, Commonwealth Secretary-General, 29 December 2000

The Commonwealth nations have a total population of 1.7 billion people and are home to about one-third of the world's young people

The Commonwealth links countries that share common historical and language connections

The Harare Declaration confirmed the Commonwealth's support for: democracy, human rights, the rule of law and good government

The Commonwealth brings countries together to tackle the following issues: promotion of sustainable development, alleviation of poverty, provision of education, protection of the environment, combating crime, fighting disease and supporting peace

TASKS

1 Why do you think the Commonwealth began?

2 What could cause some countries to be expelled or have their membership suspended?

3 Look at the map of Commonwealth countries. Are there any people in your class with links to any of these countries? Which ones?

4 Make a list of some of the activities the Commonwealth undertakes.

5 What are the advantages of the Commonwealth?

6 Can you think of any disadvantages of the Commonwealth?

Britain and the United Nations

188 countries are part of the United Nations.

Structure of the United Nations

General Assembly
Representatives of all member states have one vote. For important decisions a two-thirds majority is needed. However, their decisions are not legally binding.

International Court of Justice
This is situated in The Hague. It settles legal disputes and gives advice and opinions to states and international organisations.

Economic and Social Council
This council's responsibilities include the promotion of higher standards of living, providing solutions to international economic and social problems, and promoting respect for human rights.

Security Council
This has primary responsibility for the maintenance of international peace and security. It is made up of 15 member states: 5 countries are permanent members (UK, Russia, USA, France and China), the 10 other members change every two years. For decisions on important matters, all five of the permanent members must agree and therefore have 'veto' power. All UN members agree to accept and carry out Security Council decisions.

Trusteeship Council
This now meets only occasionally, as there are no Trust Territories left. It was originally set up to supervise very small countries, helping them develop towards independence.

Secretariat
The administrative arm of the UN headed by the Secretary-General who is appointed by the General Assembly on the recommendation of the Security Council.

History

1941
Franklin D Roosevelt and Winston Churchill signed the Atlantic **Charter**. This put forward a set of principles under which countries will work together for peace and security.

1944
Proposals for a United Nations Charter drawn up by representatives from China, the Soviet Union, the United Kingdom and the United States.

1945
Charter finalised by representatives from 50 countries at the United Nations Conference on International Organisation.
United Nations officially comes into existence having been ratified by several governments.

10 January 1946
First General Assembly held at Westminster, London.

17 January 1946
First meeting of Security Council.

1948
The General Assembly adopted the **Universal Declaration of Human Rights**.

1975
First UN conference on women.

1992
Largest ever intergovernmental conference – the "Earth Summit" to discuss the environment.

The United Nations has no army – governments voluntarily supply troops and other personnel to try to keep peace in conflict situations

The United Nations relies exclusively on member countries for funding and is not allowed to borrow money from banks

The United Nations has a number of agencies and programmes such as UNICEF (the United Nations Children's Fund), WHO (the World Health Organisation) and UNHCR (Office of the United Nations High Commissioner for Refugees)

'The United Nations remains the only global institution whose legitimacy is based on its virtually universal membership ... the only institution whose influence derives not from the use of power but from the force of the values it represents', spoken by Louise Fréchette, Deputy Secretary-General, 12 April 2001

TASKS

1 Why do you think Churchill and Roosevelt signed the Atlantic Charter in 1941, but the United Nations did not come into being until 1945?

2 What makes the United Nations different from the EU and Commonwealth?

3 Are all countries equal in the United Nations? Explain your answer.

4 Make a list of some of the activities the United Nations undertakes.

5 What are the advantages of the United Nations?

6 Can you think of any disadvantages of the United Nations?

Aims of the UN

(1) Maintain international peace and security.

(2) Develop friendly relations among nations.

(3) Promote social progress, better living standards and human rights.

ACTIVITY: CHAPTER REVIEW

1 Can you think of any other international organisations of which Britain is a member?

2 Using all the examples in this chapter, and any other information you have found out, list five of the most important benefits of Britain's membership of these organisations.

3 Explain why you have chosen these five as the most important. Share your answers with others in the class. Have a whole-class discussion about these benefits.

4 How would Britain be different if none of these links existed?

Planning Your Project

A big part of being active and effective citizens is being informed about complex issues and informing others. When people are clear about issues, they are more likely to want to take action and also more likely to actually do something about it. Being a responsible citizen can include educating other people about issues you care about. This can be the first step to creating change.

Use the information in the chapters through the book and the additional websites in the next few pages to plan your own education campaign for your school about an issue you care about. You could include posters, leaflets, an assembly, a video and a wide variety of other approaches to get your message across effectively. Think about the following issues and then decide how you are going to plan your project:

(1) Who is your project aimed at?

Depending on the age group you decide to work with you may decide that different styles of presenting information are more appropriate.

Younger students might prefer to have information presented in assemblies or through drama. Perhaps there will be students in year 7 who are not very strong readers and you do not want to put them off by producing lots of information to read.

What methods do you think would suit year 7 best?

Older students might want a more serious approach and might be more able to read more information. You will also have to think about what they have already studied in other subjects and if there are any links between what you want to say and what they may have already studied.

What methods would be more suitable for key stage 4 students?

(2) How will you get your message across?

If you are thinking of working with one particular class you may have to use very different methods than working across the whole school.

What can you do in a class that you could not do across the whole school?

What methods would be most suitable for a whole school campaign?

(3) What do you want people to know?

You may have found out a lot of information but you will have to think carefully about the key ideas or central message you want to get across to others. Before you plan your activities write down what the main points are and why you think they are the most important ideas to get across. Review your finished project and make sure your main points are still as clear as when you began the work.

If people are particularly interested and want more information, they can always follow up other sources of information themselves.

(4) Who can help you?

There are many sources of support and help. Teachers and other students may have similar interests and be keen to help out. There will also be resources you can use - the IT facilities in school, the photocopier machines, video cameras etc. There may also be local groups who can help you by providing expertise or resources or even money to help you out. It is worth checking this out before you create your own project, it may save time and effort if other people have done similar things.

Remember, campaigns around the school will need to be planned with staff so that everyone is happy for them to happen, they fit with school policy and they are coordinated - it would be confusing if a dozen campaigns started at the same time.

2 Rights and responsibilities
Police powers of stop and search

The courts
Young offenders – crime patterns and consequences

www.blink.org.uk/legal/stpsrch.htm
Stop and Search figures for Westminster

www.police.uk
The police services of the UK

www.youth-justice-board.gov.uk
The Youth Justice Board for England and Wales is helping rebuild communities and promote decent opportunities for all by preventing offending by children and young people

www.audit-commission.gov.uk
There is general information here on crime and other areas of government spending. This website also contains an audit on 'Misspent Youth' – Young People and Crime. Add the following information to the end of the website address
/ac2/NR/Police/ebla1196.htm

www.met.police.uk
The Metropolitan Police website

3 Diversity
The differences and similarities between the four nations of the UK: one nation or four?

www.scottish.parliament.uk
Website for the Scottish Parliament with information on parliament, assemblies, MSPs, parliamentary buildings and what's happening

www.scottishsecretary.gov.uk
The website of the Scotland Office. It is the Government department charged with ensuring that Scottish interests are represented within the United Kingdom Government

www.ukonline.gov.uk
Aims to tell you all you need to know about government

www.charter88.org.uk
Organisation that believes in the decentralisation of the UK, devolution, democracy, politics and reform of the constitution.

www.ni-assembly.gov.uk
Here you will find information on the work of the Northern Ireland Assembly

www.nio.gov.uk
The Northern Ireland Office is the office of the Secretary of State for Northern Ireland

www.wales.gov.uk
The website of the National Assembly for Wales

4 Government services
Taxes and spending

What types of taxes are there, how does the government raise money, what does it spend it on?

www.hm-treasury.gov.uk
Official government treasury site

www.number-10.gov.uk
Number 10 Downing Street website

www.inlandrevenue.gov.uk
Inland revenue website, featuring news and information on tax and national insurance matters in the United Kingdom

www.uktax.demon.co.uk
The UK Taxation Directory, an independently compiled catalogue of websites and material on UK tax matters

www.hmce.gov.uk
Her Majesty's Customs and Excise website

www.financialmail.co.uk
Daily Mail financial section

5 Democracy
Westminster politics

www.open.gov.uk
Government information

www.parliament.uk
Official House of Commons website

www.politicos.co.uk
Political resource centre with an MP search engine

www.ukpol.co.uk
MP biographies and information on political issues

www.annwiddecombemp.com
Homepage for Ann Widdecombe MP

www.sedgefieldlabour.org.uk
Tony Blair's constituency website

www.charleskennedy.org.uk
Charles Kennedy's website

6 Voluntary groups
Charities

Why we get involved
What charities do

www.adviceguide.co.uk
Aims to be a comprehensive resource for those people seeking help and support from charitable and voluntary organisations in the UK by trying to bring together all the providers of the help and support on one site

www.studentzone.org.uk
Contains informative section on charities and campaigns, especially for students. Enter 'charity' in the search engine

www.givingtoday.org
The Charities Aid Foundation has details about giving and a page of interesting facts

www.hands-on-helping.co.uk
This website encourages employees to donate money directly to charities from their pay packets

7 Conflict
Dealing with conflict in the workplace

Getting your rights as a consumer

www.tradingstandards.gov.uk
A one-stop shop for consumer protection information in the UK

www.ncc.org.uk
The National Consumer Council

www.netconsumer.co.uk
Review of website, links to other information, feedback and a discussion forum

www.bbc.co.uk/watchdog
Online site for the TV programme 'Watchdog'. This deals with consumer complaints

www.tuc.org.uk
The Trades Union Congress website has information about the history of trade unions and lists of all unions in the country.

www.workplaceviolence.co.uk
General information on workplace violence

www.workplace-mediation.co.uk
Mediation training courses – the site has some interesting case studies

8 The media and you
Advertising

What techniques do people use to persuade us through advertising?
The role of the media and soaps in young people's lives and development

www.culture.gov.uk/creative
Government site for Creative, Media, and Arts TV and Media as well as commercial TV and radio

www.adassoc.org.uk
The Advertising Association website has information about their members and a quiz

www.media-awareness.ca
This Canadian website has lots of information and ideas about media culture

www.asa.org.uk
The Advertising Standards Authority website: this has the rules advertisers are supposed to follow

9 Global community
EU, Commonwealth and the UN – how are we linked to other countries?
What do we gain from those links?

www.cec.org.uk
The European Commission Representation in the UK

www.europarl.org.uk
UK Office of the European Parliament

www.europarl.eu.int
The multilingual Web server of the European Parliament

www.fco.gov.uk
Information on the EU, UN and Commonwealth

www.europa.eu.int
European Union general site on free movement and the rights of a citizen

www.un.org
United Nations website

www.commonwealth.org.uk
Information on the Commonwealth and Commonwealth Institute in London

Glossary

Bill – the name given to a draft law before it is passed by Parliament. A bill can change as it is discussed in the Houses of Parliament. Once it has been accepted, the bill becomes an Act of Law

Charter – written description of what an organisation is for and how it will work

Civil service – the part of government that carries out the administration i.e. the planning, monitoring, reporting, etc.

Colony – an area or country which is controlled by another country: for example, India was a colony of Britain

Common denominator – something that we all have in common

Compassion – helping people through feelings of sympathy

Conflict – disagreement between different interests

Confrontation – a situation in which people deal with differences of opinion face to face

Consensus – agreement

Constituency – the area that elects one MP, some large towns are divided into several constituencies.

Consumer – customer

Court of Appeal – a higher court you can go to have your case reconsidered

Donation – gift of money or something else to a charity

Duties – taxes on certain kinds of products, especially imports.

The Establishment – this refers to the group of people and organisations who run the country

Expenditure – spending

Gender – a person's sex, male or female

Imperial – anything which is part of an 'empire', ie a collection of countries ruled by one

Indictable offence – something for which a person can be charged

Judiciary – all judges

Labour – work

Manifesto – the list of promises political parties make before elections about what they will do if they become the next government.

MP – Member of Parliament, the elected representatives of the House of Commons

MEP – Member of the European Parliament

Monarch – a King or Queen

Press secretary – someone who deals with journalists on behalf of the government

Redundancies – this refers to workers being laid off when their job is no longer required by the employer. This is different from being 'sacked', which is linked to poor performance in a job.

Republican – someone who does not want a monarchy

Retailer – seller, for example, a shop or catalogue

Strike – workers refuse to work in order to put pressure on employers to accept their demands

Treaty – an agreement between countries

United Nations Declaration of Human Rights – the list of individual rights the UN tries to protect

Volunteer – someone who gives up his or her time to work without payment

Westminster – the area in London where Parliament is located. People often refer to Westminster when they mean Parliament.

Index

COLOR BLOCK

quilts

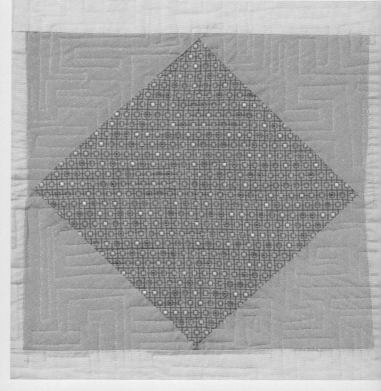

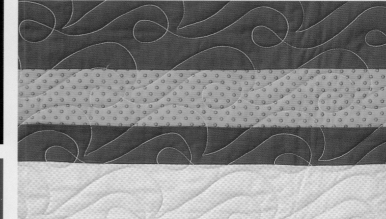

LEISURE ARTS, INC.
Little Rock, Arkansas

ISBN-13: 978-1-46470-054-5

TABLE OF CONTENTS

COLOR BLOCK
QUILTS

Vivid contrasts and large fabric pieces make these color block quilts exciting to see—and a snap to sew! Judith McCabe created these patterns to be fuss-free and fast to finish. The contemporary designs truly are perfect for the beginning quilter, while the experienced quilter will enjoy the exhilaration of achieving almost instant results. Whatever your skill level, these designs will add new energy to your home décor. The quilts look amazing when draped over a chair, hung on the wall, or spread over a table. And they're wonderful as quick and thoughtful gifts!

ABOUT
JUDITH McCABE

Originally from New Jersey, designer Judith McCabe now lives in Lancaster County, Pennsylvania. She says, "You can't live here and be unaware of the beauty of quilts. They're everywhere, and after a while they inspired me to try my hand at quilting."

No stranger to needle and thread, Judith credits her mother for teaching her to sew. "As children, my sisters and I all had access to sewing supplies and fabric scraps to practice our stitches. We still love to be creative, doing crochet, sewing, or needlework. Designing needlework has been my primary interest for several years. However, working with fabric seems to allow more freedom to experiment with color, which I enjoy.

"I think that today's quilters are looking for projects they can complete quickly. That's what I had in mind when creating these designs. These quilts are fast to finish, colorful, and will be used and loved for years to come."

LADDERS

Finished Quilt Size: 82¼" x 94¾" (209 cm x 241 cm)

FABRIC REQUIREMENTS

Yardage is based on 43"/44" (109 cm/112 cm) wide fabric with a usable width of 40" (102 cm).

- 5½ yds (5 m) of dark grey solid (includes binding)
- 1⅞ yds (1.7 m) of light grey solid
- 1 yd (91 cm) of blue tonal
- 7½ yds (6.9 m) of fabric for backing

You will also need:

- 90" x 103" (229 cm x 262 cm) piece of batting

CUTTING THE PIECES

*Follow **Rotary Cutting**, page 38, to cut fabric. Cut all strips from the selvage-to-selvage width unless otherwise noted. All measurements include ¼" seam allowances.*

From dark grey solid:
- Cut 6 *lengthwise* **setting strips** 9½" x 94½".
- Cut 4 *lengthwise* **binding strips** 2¼" x 94½".

From light grey solid:
- Cut 10 strips 6" wide. From these strips, cut 5 **large rectangles** 6" x 15", 25 **medium rectangles** 6" x 8½", and 5 **small rectangles** 6" x 7".

From blue tonal:
- Cut 5 strips 6" wide. From these strips, cut 30 **squares** 6" x 6".

MAKING THE QUILT TOP

Follow **Piecing** *and* **Pressing**, *page 39, to make quilt top.*

1. Sew 5 **medium rectangles** and 6 **squares** together to make **Unit 1.** Make 5 Unit 1's.

Unit 1 (make 5)

2. Sew 1 **small rectangle**, 1 **Unit 1**, and 1 **large rectangle** together to make *vertical* **Row.** Make 5 Rows.

Row (make 5)

3. Referring to **Quilt Top Diagram**, sew **Rows** and **setting strips** together to make quilt top.

COMPLETING THE QUILT

1. Follow **Quilting**, page 40, to mark, layer, and quilt as desired. Quilt shown is machine quilted with meandering quilting.
2. Follow **Making a Hanging Sleeve**, page 43, if a hanging sleeve is desired.
3. Use **binding strips** and follow **Binding**, page 44, to bind quilt.

Quilt Top Diagram

LADDERS Version 2
Finished Quilt Size: 49¼" x 44¾" (125 cm x 114 cm)

FABRIC REQUIREMENTS

Yardage is based on 43"/44" (109 cm/112 cm) wide fabric with a usable width of 40" (102 cm).

- 1⅜ yds (1.3 m) of black solid
- ⅞ yd (80 cm) of white/black print (includes binding)
- ¼ yd (23 cm) of red solid
- 3 yds (2.7 m) of fabric for backing

You will also need:

- 57" x 53" (145 cm x 135 cm) piece of batting

CUTTING THE PIECES

Follow **Rotary Cutting**, *page 38, to cut fabric. Cut all strips from the selvage-to-selvage width unless otherwise noted. All measurements include ¼" seam allowances.*

From black solid:
- Cut 4 *lengthwise* **setting strips** 10" x 44½".

From white/black print:
- Cut 6 **binding strips** 2¼" wide.
- Cut 3 strips 4" wide. From these strips, cut 12 **rectangles** 4" x 8".

From red solid:
- Cut 2 strips 4" wide. From these strips, cut 12 **squares** 4" x 4".

MAKING THE QUILT TOP

Follow **Piecing** *and* **Pressing**, *page 39, to make quilt top.*

1. Sew 4 **rectangles** and 4 **squares** together to make *vertical* **Row.** Make 3 Rows.

Row (make 3)

2. Referring to photo, sew **Rows** and **setting strips** together to make quilt top.

COMPLETING THE QUILT

1. Follow **Quilting**, page 40, to mark, layer, and quilt as desired. Quilt shown is machine quilted with an all-over loop pattern.
2. Follow **Making a Hanging Sleeve**, page 43, if a hanging sleeve is desired.
3. Use **binding strips** and follow **Binding**, page 44, to bind quilt.

DIAMOND

Finished Quilt Size: 54³/₄" x 60³/₄" (139 cm x 154 cm)

FABRIC REQUIREMENTS

Yardage is based on 43"/44" (109 cm/112 cm) wide fabric with a usable width of 40" (102 cm).

- 2 yds (1.8 m) of black solid (includes binding)
- 2 yds (1.8 m) of teal solid
- ⁵/₈ yd (57 cm) of teal tonal
- 3⁷/₈ yds (3.5 m) of fabric for backing

You will also need:

- 63" x 69" (160 cm x 175 cm) piece of batting

CUTTING THE PIECES

Follow **Rotary Cutting**, *page 38, to cut fabric. Cut all strips from the selvage-to-selvage width unless otherwise noted. Cutting lengths for borders are exact. All measurements include ¹/₄" seam allowances.*

From black solid:

- Cut 7 **binding strips** 2¹/₄" wide.
- Cut 2 lengthwise **side outer borders** 6" x 49¹/₂".
- Cut 2 lengthwise **top/bottom outer borders** 6" x 43¹/₂".

From remainder of width,

- Cut 2 squares 13¹/₄" x 13¹/₄". Cut squares *once* diagonally to make 4 **triangles**.

From teal solid:

- Cut 2 **side inner borders** 9⁵/₈" x 25¹/₄".
- Cut 2 lengthwise **top/bottom inner borders** 12⁵/₈" x 43¹/₂".

From teal tonal:

- Cut 1 **center square** 18" x 18".

From remainder of width,

- Cut 2 strips 6" wide. From these strips, cut 4 **corner squares** 6" x 6".

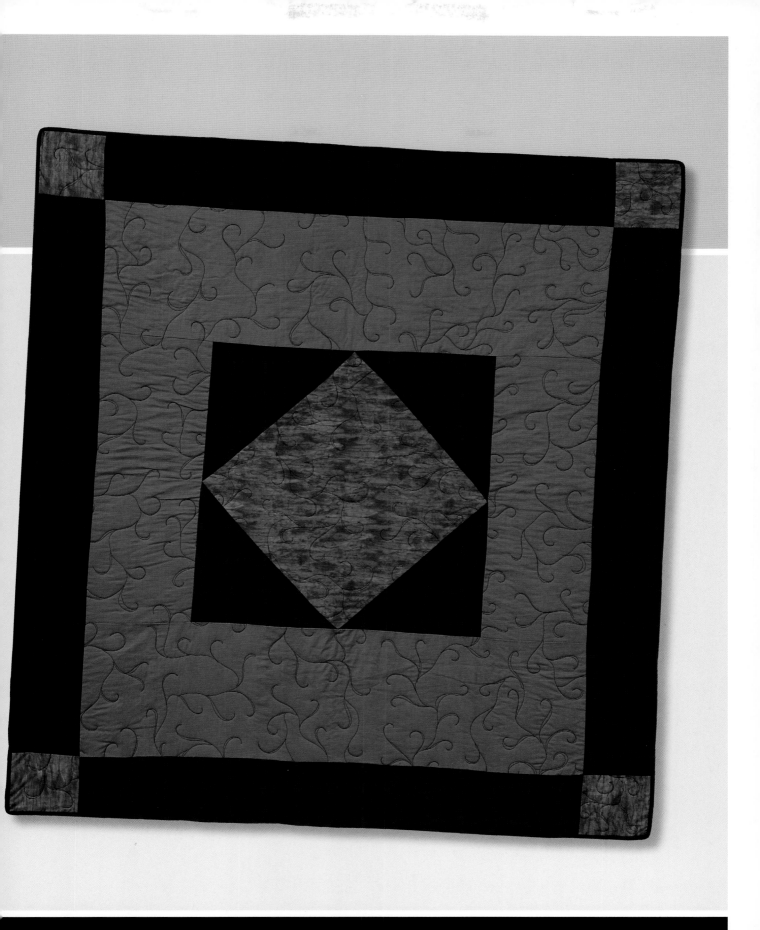

MAKING THE QUILT TOP

*Follow **Piecing** and **Pressing**, page 39, to make quilt top.*

1. Sew 2 **triangles** to opposite sides of **center square** (**Fig. 1**).

Fig. 1

2. Sew 2 **triangles** to remaining sides of center square to make **Diamond Unit**.

Diamond Unit

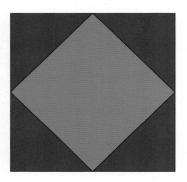

3. Referring to **Quilt Top Diagram**, match centers and corners and sew **side inner borders** to Diamond Unit.
4. Matching centers and corners, sew **top/bottom inner borders** to Diamond Unit.
5. Matching centers and corners, sew **side outer borders** to quilt top.
6. Sew 1 **corner square** to each end of **top/bottom outer borders**.
7. Matching centers and corners, sew **top/bottom outer borders** to quilt top.

COMPLETING THE QUILT

1. Follow **Quilting**, page 40, to mark, layer, and quilt as desired. Quilt shown is machine quilted with an all-over vine pattern.
2. Follow **Making a Hanging Sleeve**, page 43, if a hanging sleeve is desired.
3. Use **binding strips** and follow **Binding**, page 44, to bind quilt.

Quilt Top Diagram

DIAMOND Version 2

Finished Quilt Size: 40³/₄" x 40³/₄" (104 cm x 104 cm)

FABRIC REQUIREMENTS

Yardage is based on 43"/44" (109 cm/112 cm) wide fabric with a usable width of 40" (102 cm).

- 1³/₈ yds (1.3 m) of yellow tonal (includes binding)
- ³/₄ yd (69 cm) of turquoise tonal
- ³/₈ yd (34 cm) of green print
- 2³/₄ yds (2.5 m) of fabric for backing

You will also need:

- 49" x 49" (124 cm x 124 cm) piece of batting

CUTTING THE PIECES

*Follow **Rotary Cutting**, page 38, to cut fabric. Cut all strips from the selvage-to-selvage width. Cutting lengths for borders are exact. All measurements include ¹/₄" seam allowances.*

From yellow tonal:
- Cut 5 **binding strips** 2¹/₄" wide.
- Cut 1 strip 10¹/₂" wide. From this strip, cut 2 **side inner borders** 10¹/₂" x 14¹/₂".
- Cut 2 **top/bottom inner borders** 10¹/₂" x 34¹/₂".

From turquoise tonal:
- Cut 2 **large rectangles** 3¹/₂" x 28¹/₂".
- Cut 2 strips 3¹/₂" wide. From these strips, cut 4 **medium rectangles** 3¹/₂" x 11³/₄" and 4 **squares** 3¹/₂" x 3¹/₂".
- Cut 2 squares 8¹/₈" x 8¹/₈". Cut squares *once* diagonally to make 4 **triangles**.

From green print:
- Cut 1 **center square** 10¹/₈" x 10¹/₈".
From remainder of width,
- Cut 2 strips 3¹/₂" wide. From these strips, cut 2 **small rectangles** 3¹/₂" x 6" and 8 **squares** 3¹/₂" x 3¹/₂".

MAKING THE QUILT TOP

*Follow **Piecing** and **Pressing**, page 39, to make quilt top.* **Note:** *The points of the triangles will overlap, causing the center square to appear to "float."*

1. Sew 2 **triangles** to opposite sides of **center square** (**Fig. 1**).

Fig. 1

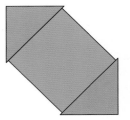

2. Sew 2 **triangles** to remaining sides of center square to make **Diamond Unit**.

Diamond Unit

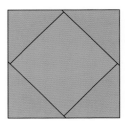

3. Referring to photo, match centers and corners and sew **side inner borders** to Diamond Unit.

4. Matching centers and corners, sew **top/bottom inner borders** to Diamond Unit.

5. Sew 1 **large rectangle** and 2 green **squares** together to make **side outer border**. Make 2 side outer borders.

6. Matching centers and corners, sew side outer borders to quilt top.

7. Sew 2 **medium rectangles**, 1 **small rectangle**, 2 green **squares**, and 2 turquoise **squares** together to make **top outer border**. Repeat to make **bottom outer border**.

8. Matching centers and corners, sew top/bottom outer borders to quilt top.

COMPLETING THE QUILT

1. Follow **Quilting**, page 40, to mark, layer, and quilt as desired. Quilt shown is machine quilted with an all-over geometric pattern.

2. Follow **Making a Hanging Sleeve**, page 43, if a hanging sleeve is desired.

3. Use **binding strips** and follow **Binding**, page 44, to bind quilt.

STACKED BLOCKS

Finished Quilt Size: 76³/₄" x 86¹/₄" (195 cm x 219 cm)

FABRIC REQUIREMENTS

Yardage is based on 43"/44" (109 cm/112 cm) wide fabric with a usable width of 40" (102 cm).

- 2¹/₄ yds (2.1 m) of black solid
- 2¹/₄ yds (2.1 m) of black print (includes binding)
- 1 yd (91 cm) of purple solid
- 1¹/₄ yds (1.1 m) of purple tonal
- ⁵/₈ yd (57 cm) of blue solid
- 7¹/₈ yds (6.5 m) of fabric for backing

You will also need:

- 85" x 94" (216 cm x 239 cm) piece of batting

CUTTING THE PIECES

Follow **Rotary Cutting**, *page 38, to cut fabric. Cut all strips from the selvage-to-selvage width. All measurements include ¹/₄" seam allowances.*

From black solid:
- Cut 7 strips 10" wide. From these strips, cut 10 **rectangles** 10" x 19¹/₂" and 5 **squares** 10" x 10".

From black print:
- Cut 9 **binding strips** 2¹/₄" wide.
- Cut 5 strips 10" wide. From these strips, cut 5 **rectangles** 10" x 19¹/₂" and 7 **squares** 10" x 10".

From purple solid:
- Cut 3 strips 10" wide. From these strips, cut 4 **rectangles** 10" x 19¹/₂" and 2 **squares** 10" x 10".

From purple tonal:
- Cut 4 strips 10" wide. From these strips, cut 5 **rectangles** 10" x 19¹/₂" and 4 **squares** 10" x 10".

From blue solid:
- Cut 2 strips 10" wide. From these strips, cut 2 **rectangles** 10" x 19¹/₂" and 2 **squares** 10" x 10".

MAKING THE QUILT TOP

*Follow **Piecing** and **Pressing**, page 39, to make quilt top.*

1. Sew 3 **rectangles** (2 black solid and 1 black print) and 2 **squares** (1 black solid and 1 purple tonal) together to make **Row A**.

Row A

2. Sew 2 **rectangles**, (1 purple solid and 1 purple tonal) and 4 **squares** (2 black solid, 1 black print, and 1 blue solid) together to make **Row B**.

Row B

3. Sew 3 **rectangles** (2 black solid and 1 black print) and 2 **squares** (1 black print and 1 purple tonal) together to make **Row C**.

Row C

4. Sew 3 **rectangles** (1 black solid, 1 black print, and 1 purple solid) and 2 **squares** (1 purple tonal and 1 blue solid) together to make **Row D**.

Row D

5. Sew 3 **rectangles** (1 black solid, 1 black print, and 1 blue solid) and 2 **squares** (1 purple solid and 1 purple tonal) together to make **Row E**.

Row E

6. Sew 3 **rectangles** (1 black solid, 1 purple solid and 1 purple tonal) and 2 **squares** (2 black print) together to make **Row F**.

Row F

7. Sew 3 **rectangles** (1 black solid, 1 black print, and 1 purple tonal) and 2 **squares** (1 black solid and 1 purple solid) together to make **Row G**.

Row G

8. Sew 3 **rectangles** (1 purple solid, 1 purple tonal, and 1 blue solid) and 2 **squares** (1 blac solid and 1 black print) together to make **Row H**.

Row H

9. Sew 3 **rectangles** (2 black solid and 1 purple tonal) and 2 **squares** (2 black print) together to make **Row I**.

Row I

10. Referring to **Quilt Top Diagram**, sew **Rows** together in alphabetical order, top to bottom, to complete quilt top.

COMPLETING THE QUILT

1. Follow **Quilting**, page 40, to mark, layer, and quilt as desired. Quilt shown is machine quilted with a continuous loop and star pattern.

2. Follow **Making a Hanging Sleeve**, page 43, if a hanging sleeve is desired.

3. Use **binding strips** and follow **Binding**, page 44, to bind quilt.

Quilt Top Diagram

STACKED BLOCKS Version 2

Finished Quilt Size: 58¼" x 69¾" (148 cm x 177 cm)

FABRIC REQUIREMENTS

Yardage is based on 43"/44" (109 cm/112 cm) wide fabric with a usable width of 40" (102 cm).

- 2⅜ yds (2.2 m) of green print (includes binding)
- ¾ yd (69 cm) of green solid
- ¾ yd (69 cm) of turquoise solid
- 1⅛ yds (1 m) of purple solid
- 4⅜ yds (4 m) of fabric for backing

You will also need:

- 66" x 78" (168 cm x 198 cm) piece of batting

CUTTING THE PIECES

*Follow **Rotary Cutting**, page 38, to cut fabric. Cut all strips from the selvage-to-selvage width. All measurements include ¼" seam allowances.*

From green print:
- Cut 7 **binding strips** 2¼" wide.
- Cut 5 strips 12" wide. From these strips, cut 5 **rectangles** 12" x 23½" and 2 **squares** 12" x 12".

From green solid:
- Cut 2 strips 12" wide. From these strips, cut 5 **squares** 12" x 12".

From turquoise solid:
- Cut 2 strips 12" wide. From these strips, cut 5 **squares** 12" x 12".

From purple solid:
- Cut 3 strips 12" wide. From these strips, cut 3 **rectangles** 12" x 23½" and 2 **squares** 12" x 12".

MAKING THE QUILT TOP

*Follow **Piecing** and **Pressing**, page 39, to make quilt top.*

1. Sew 1 **rectangle** (purple solid) and 3 **squares** (1 green print, 1 green solid, and 1 turquoise solid) together to make **Row A**.

Row A

2. Sew 1 **rectangle** (purple solid) and 3 **squares** (1 green print, 1 green solid, and 1 purple solid) together to make **Row B**.

Row B

3. Sew 1 **rectangle** (green print) and 3 **squares** (2 green solid and 1 turquoise solid) together to make **Row C**.

Row C

4. Sew 2 **rectangles** (1 green print and 1 purple solid) and 1 **square** (turquoise solid) together to make **Row D**.

Row D

5. Sew 1 **rectangle** (green print) and 3 **squares** (1 green solid, 1 turquoise solid, and 1 purple solid) together to make **Row E**.

Row E

6. Sew 2 **rectangles** (2 green print) and 1 **square** (turquoise solid) together to make **Row F**.

Row F

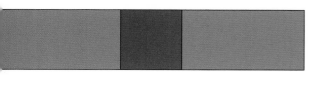

7. Referring to photo, sew **Rows** together in alphabetical order, top to bottom, to complete quilt top.

COMPLETING THE QUILT

1. Follow **Quilting**, page 40, to mark, layer, and quilt as desired. Quilt shown is machine quilted with an all-over ribbon pattern.

2. Follow **Making a Hanging Sleeve**, page 43, if a hanging sleeve is desired.

3. Use **binding strips** and follow **Binding**, page 44, to bind quilt.

VERTICAL STRIPS

Finished Quilt Size: 58¼" x 58¼" (148 cm x 148 cm)

FABRIC REQUIREMENTS

Yardage is based on 43"/44" (109 cm/112 cm) wide fabric with a usable width of 40" (102 cm).

- 1½ yds (1.4 m) of light grey solid (includes binding)
- 1½ yds (1.4 m) of dark grey solid
- 1½ yds (1.4 m) of grey tonal
- 3¾ yds (3.4 m) of fabric for backing

You will also need:

- 66" x 66" (168 cm x 168 cm) piece of batting

CUTTING THE PIECES

Follow **Rotary Cutting**, *page 38, to cut fabric. Cut all strips from the selvage-to-selvage width unless otherwise noted. Cutting lengths for borders are exact. All measurements include ¼" seam allowances.*

From light grey solid:
- Cut 4 *lengthwise* **borders** 6" x 47".
- Cut 6 *lengthwise* **binding strips** 2¼" x 47".

From dark grey solid:
- Cut 4 *lengthwise* **wide strips** 8" x 47".

From grey tonal:
- Cut 3 *lengthwise* **narrow strips** 6" x 47".

From remainder of width,
- Cut 2 strips 6" wide. From these strips, cut 4 **corner squares** 6" x 6".

MAKING THE QUILT TOP

*Follow **Piecing** and **Pressing**, page 39, to make quilt top.*

1. Referring to **Quilt Top Diagram**, sew dark grey **wide strips** and grey tonal **narrow strips** together to make quilt top center.
2. Matching centers and corners, sew 2 **borders** to sides of quilt top center.
3. Sew 1 **corner square** to *each* end of remaining **borders**. Matching centers, seams, and corners, sew borders to top and bottom of quilt top center.

COMPLETING THE QUILT

1. Follow **Quilting**, page 40, to mark, layer, and quilt as desired. Quilt shown is machine quilted with meandering quilting.
2. Follow **Making a Hanging Sleeve**, page 43, if a hanging sleeve is desired.
3. Use **binding strips** and follow **Binding**, page 44, to bind quilt.

Quilt Top Diagram

VERTICAL STRIPS Version 2
Finished Quilt Size: 33" x 50³/₄" (84 cm x 129 cm)

FABRIC REQUIREMENTS

Yardage is based on 43"/44" (109 cm/112 cm) wide fabric with a usable width of 40" (102 cm).

1³/₈ yds (1.3 m) of purple print (includes binding)

1³/₈ yds (1.3 m) of purple solid

1³/₈ yds (1.3 m) of fuchsia solid

1³/₈ yds (1.3 m) of scarlet tonal

3³/₈ yds (3.1 m)* of fabric for backing

You will also need:

41" x 59" (104 cm x 150 cm) piece of batting

*If usable width of fabric is 41" or more, one length (1³/₄ yds [1.6 m]) will be adequate.

CUTTING THE PIECES

*Follow **Rotary Cutting**, page 38, to cut fabric. Cutting lengths for borders are exact. All measurements include ¹/₄" seam allowances.*

From purple print:
- Cut 2 *lengthwise* **wide strips** 6¹/₄" x 45".
- Cut 5 *lengthwise* **binding strips** 2¹/₄" x 45".

From purple solid:
- Cut 1 *lengthwise* **center strip** 3¹/₄" x 45".
- Cut 2 *lengthwise* **side borders** 3¹/₄" x 45".
- Cut 2 *lengthwise* **top/bottom borders** 3¹/₄" x 32³/₄".

From fuchsia solid:
- Cut 2 *lengthwise* **narrow strips** 3¹/₄" x 45".

From scarlet tonal:
- Cut 2 *lengthwise* **medium strips** 4" x 45".

MAKING THE QUILT TOP

*Follow **Piecing** and **Pressing**, page 39, to make quilt top.*

1. Referring to photo, sew **wide**, **medium**, **narrow**, and **center strips** together to make quilt top center.
2. Matching centers and corners, sew **side borders** to quilt top center.
3. Matching centers and corners, sew **top/bottom borders** to quilt top center.

COMPLETING THE QUILT

1. Follow **Quilting**, page 40, to mark, layer, and quilt as desired. Quilt shown is machine quilted with an all-over ribbon pattern.
2. Follow **Making a Hanging Sleeve**, page 43, if a hanging sleeve is desired.
3. Use **binding strips** and follow **Binding**, page 44, to bind quilt.

VERTICAL ROWS

Finished Quilt Size: 33¼" x 42¾" (84 cm x 109 cm)

FABRIC REQUIREMENTS

Yardage is based on 43"/44" (109 cm/112 cm) wide fabric with a usable width of 40" (102 cm).

- 1⅜ yds (1.3 m) of black solid
- ½ yd (46 cm) of black with gold flecks (includes binding)
- ¼ yd (23 cm) of black print
- ⅛ yd (11 cm) *each* of cream solid and green solid
- 2⅞ yds (2.6 m)* of fabric for backing

You will also need:

- 41" x 51" (104 cm x 130 cm) piece of batting

*If usable width of fabric is 41" or more, one length (1½ yds [1.4 m]) will be adequate.

CUTTING THE PIECES

*Follow **Rotary Cutting**, page 38, to cut fabric. Cut all strips from the selvage-to-selvage width unless otherwise noted. All measurements include ¼" seam allowances.*

From black solid:
- Cut 4 *lengthwise* **setting strips** 6" x 42½" wide.

From black with gold flecks:
- Cut 5 **binding strips** 2¼" wide.
- Cut 1 strip 4" wide. From this strip, cut 4 **small rectangles** 4" x 7½".

From black print:
- Cut 2 strips 4" wide. From these strips, cut 2 **large rectangles** 4" x 14½" and 4 **small rectangles** 4" x 7½".

From *each* of cream solid and green solid:
- Cut 1 strip 4" wide. From this strip, cut 6 **squares** 4" x 4".

MAKING THE QUILT TOP

*Follow **Piecing** and **Pressing**, page 39, to make quilt top.*

1. Sew 2 black with gold flecks **small rectangles**, 2 black print **small rectangles**, and 1 black print **large rectangle** together to make *vertical* **Row A**. Make 2 Row A's.

Row A (make 2)

2. Sew 6 cream **squares** and 6 green squares together to make *vertical* **Row B**.

Row B

3. Referring to **Quilt Top Diagram**, sew **Row A's**, **Row B**, and **setting strips** together to make quilt top.

COMPLETING THE QUILT

1. Follow **Quilting**, page 40, to mark, layer, and quilt as desired. Quilt shown is machine quilted with meandering quilting.

2. Follow **Making a Hanging Sleeve**, page 43, if a hanging sleeve is desired.

3. Use **binding strips** and follow **Binding**, page 44, to bind quilt.

Quilt Top Diagram

VERTICAL ROWS Version 2

Finished Quilt Size: 54³/₄" x 54³/₄" (139 cm x 139 cm)

FABRIC REQUIREMENTS

Yardage is based on 43"/44" (109 cm/112 cm) wide fabric with a usable width of 40" (102 cm).

   2¹/₈ yds (1.9 m) of light blue print (includes binding)
   ⁵/₈ yd (57 cm) of dark blue solid
   ¹/₂ yd (46 cm) of yellow tonal
   ¹/₄ yd (23 cm) of turquoise tonal
   3¹/₂ yds (3.2 m) of fabric for backing
You will also need:
   63" x 63" (160 cm x 160 cm) piece of batting

CUTTING THE PIECES

Follow **Rotary Cutting**, *page 38, to cut fabric. Cut all strips from the selvage-to-selvage width unless otherwise noted. All measurements include ¹/₄" seam allowances.*

From light blue print:
- Cut 6 **binding strips** 2¹/₄" wide.
- Cut 4 *lengthwise* **setting strips** 9¹/₂" x 54¹/₂" wide.

From dark blue solid:
- Cut 2 strips 6¹/₂" wide. From these strips, cut 8 **rectangles** 6¹/₂" x 9¹/₂".
- Cut 1 strip 6¹/₂" wide. From this strip, cut 3 **squares** 6¹/₂" x 6¹/₂".

From yellow tonal:
- Cut 1 strip 6¹/₂" wide. From this strip, cut 4 **rectangles** 6¹/₂" x 9¹/₂".
- Cut 1 strip 6¹/₂" wide. From this strip, cut 3 **squares** 6¹/₂" x 6¹/₂".

From turquoise tonal:
- Cut 1 strip 6¹/₂" wide. From this strip, cut 3 **squares** 6¹/₂" x 6¹/₂".

MAKING THE QUILT TOP

Follow **Piecing** *and* **Pressing**, *page 39, to make quilt top.*

1. Sew 4 dark blue **rectangles** and 2 yellow **rectangles** together to make *vertical* **Row A**. Make 2 Row A's.

Row A (make 2)

2. Sew 3 dark blue **squares**, 3 yellow **squares**, and 3 turquoise **squares** together to make *vertical* **Row B**.

Row B

3. Referring to photo, sew **Row A's**, **Row B**, and **setting strips** together to make quilt top.

COMPLETING THE QUILT

1. Follow **Quilting**, page 40, to mark, layer, and quilt as desired. Quilt shown is machine quilted with an all-over loop pattern.
2. Follow **Making a Hanging Sleeve**, page 43, if a hanging sleeve is desired.
3. Use **binding strips** and follow **Binding**, page 44, to bind quilt.

HORIZONTAL STRIPS

Finished Quilt Size: 30³/₄" x 42³/₄" (78 cm x 109 cm)

FABRIC REQUIREMENTS

Yardage is based on 43"/44" (109 cm/112 cm) wide fabric with a usable width of 40" (102 cm).

- 1¹/₈ yds (1 m) of brown solid (includes binding)
- ³/₈ yd (34 cm) of tan tonal
- ³/₈ yd (34 cm) of orange solid
- ³/₈ yd (34 cm) of yellow print
- 1¹/₂ yds (1.4 m) of fabric for backing

You will also need:

- 39" x 51" (99 cm x 130 cm) piece of batting

CUTTING THE PIECES

*Follow **Rotary Cutting**, page 38, to cut fabric. Cut all strips from the selvage-to-selvage width. Cutting lengths for borders are exact. All measurements include ¹/₄" seam allowances.* **Tip:** *Label each strip with corresponding letter as you cut.*

From brown solid:
- Cut 5 **binding strips** 2¹/₄" wide.
- Cut 1 *each* of **strips B**, **E**, and **H** 2¹/₄" x 22¹/₂".
- Cut 2 **side borders** 4¹/₂" x 34¹/₂".
- Cut 2 **top/bottom borders** 4¹/₂" x 30¹/₂".

From tan tonal:
- Cut 1 **strip A** 6¹/₄" x 22¹/₂".
- Cut 1 **strip F** 4¹/₄" x 22¹/₂".

From orange solid:
- Cut 1 **strip C** 4¹/₄" x 22¹/₂".
- Cut 1 **strip I** 6¹/₄" x 22¹/₂".

From yellow print:
- Cut 1 **strip D** 6¹/₄" x 22¹/₂".
- Cut 1 **strip G** 4¹/₂" x 22¹/₂".

MAKING THE QUILT TOP

Follow **Piecing** *and* **Pressing**, *page 39, to make quilt top.*

1. Referring to **Quilt Top Diagram**, sew **strips A-I** together in alphabetical order to make quilt top center.
2. Matching centers and corners, sew **side borders** to quilt top center.
3. Matching centers and corners, sew **top/bottom borders** to quilt top center.

COMPLETING THE QUILT

1. Follow **Quilting**, page 40, to mark, layer, and quilt as desired. Quilt shown is machine quilted with an all-over pattern.
2. Follow **Making a Hanging Sleeve**, page 43, if a hanging sleeve is desired.
3. Use **binding strips** and follow **Binding**, page 44, to bind quilt.

Quilt Top Diagram

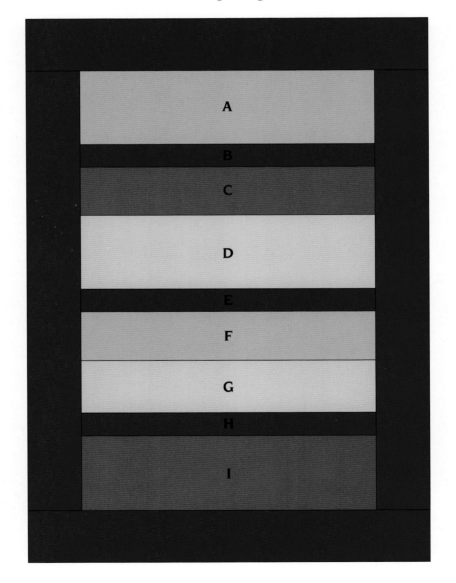

HORIZONTAL STRIPS Version 2

Finished Quilt Size: 42³/₄" x 56³/₄" (109 cm x 144 cm)

FABRIC REQUIREMENTS

Yardage is based on 43"/44" (109 cm/112 cm) wide fabric with a usable width of 40" (102 cm).

- 2 yds (1.8 m) of red solid (includes binding)
- ¼ yd (23 cm) of plum tonal
- ³/₈ yd (34 cm) of pink dot
- ³/₈ yd (34 cm) of light pink print
- ½ yd (46 cm) of medium pink print
- 3⁵/₈ yds (3.3 m) of fabric for backing

You will also need:

- 51" x 65" (130 cm x 165 cm) piece of batting

CUTTING THE PIECES

Follow **Rotary Cutting**, *page 38, to cut fabric. Cut all strips from the selvage-to-selvage width unless otherwise noted. Cutting lengths for borders are exact. All measurements include ¼" seam allowances.* **Tip:** *Label each strip with corresponding letter as you cut.*

From red solid:
- Cut 6 **binding strips** 2¼" wide.
- Cut 1 **strip B** 2" x 30½.
- Cut 1 **strip G** 2¼" x 30½.
- Cut 1 **strip J** 2¼" x 30½.
- Cut 2 *lengthwise* **side borders** 6½" x 44½".
- Cut 2 *lengthwise* **top/bottom borders** 6½" x 42½".

From plum tonal:
- Cut 1 **strip F** 3³/₄" x 30½".
- Cut 1 **strip N** 1³/₄" x 30½".

From pink dot:
- Cut 1 **strip A** 3" x 30½".
- Cut 1 **strip E** 4½" x 30½".
- Cut 1 **strip M** 3³/₄" x 30½".

From light pink print:
- Cut 1 **strip C** 4½" x 30½".
- Cut 1 **strip H** 2³/₄" x 30½".
- Cut 1 **strip L** 4³/₄" x 30½".

From medium pink print:
- Cut 1 **strip D** 6½" x 30½".
- Cut 1 **strip I** 6½" x 30½".
- Cut 1 **strip K** 2³/₄" x 30½".

MAKING THE QUILT TOP

Follow **Piecing** *and* **Pressing**, *page 39, to make quilt top.*

1. Referring to photo, sew **strips A-N** together in alphabetical order to make quilt top center.
2. Matching centers and corners, sew **side borders** to quilt top center.
3. Matching centers and corners, sew **top/ bottom borders** to quilt top center.

COMPLETING THE QUILT

1. Follow **Quilting**, page 40, to mark, layer, and quilt as desired. Quilt shown is machine quilted with alternating looping and curving lines quilted from side to side of quilt.
2. Follow **Making a Hanging Sleeve**, page 43, if a hanging sleeve is desired.
3. Use **binding strips** and follow **Binding**, page 44, to bind quilt.

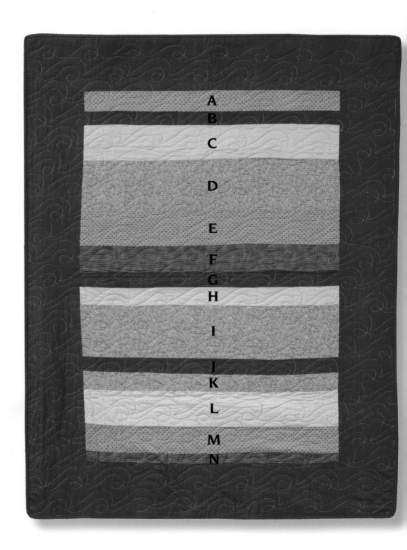

GENERAL INSTRUCTIONS

To make your quilting easier and more enjoyable, we encourage you to carefully read all of the general instructions, study the color photographs, and familiarize yourself with the individual project instructions before beginning a project.

FABRICS

SELECTING FABRICS

Choose high-quality, medium-weight 100% cotton fabrics. All-cotton fabrics hold a crease better, fray less, and are easier to quilt than cotton/polyester blends.

Yardage requirements listed for each project are based on 43"/44" wide fabric with a "usable" width of 40" after shrinkage and trimming selvages. Actual usable width will probably vary slightly from fabric to fabric. Our recommended yardage lengths should be adequate for occasional re-squaring of fabric when many cuts are required.

PREPARING FABRICS

We recommend that fabrics be washed, dried, and pressed before cutting. If fabrics are not pre-washed, washing the finished quilt may cause shrinkage and may cause the dyes in darker fabrics to bleed onto lighter fabrics. After washing and drying fabric, fold lengthwise with wrong sides together and selvages matching.

ROTARY CUTTING

- Place fabric on work surface with fold closest to you.

- Cut all strips from the selvage-to-selvage width of the fabric unless otherwise indicated in project instructions.

- Square left edge of fabric using rotary cutter and rulers (**Figs. 1-2**).

- To cut each strip required for a project, place ruler over cut edge of fabric, aligning desired marking on ruler with cut edge; make cut (**Fig. 3**).

- When cutting several strips from a single piece of fabric, it is important to make sure that cuts remain at a perfect right angle to the fold; square fabric as needed.

Fig. 1

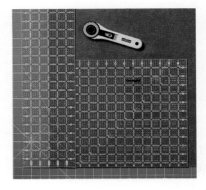

Fig. 2

Fig. 3

PIECING

- Set sewing machine stitch length for approximately 11 stitches per inch.

- Use neutral-colored general-purpose sewing thread (not quilting thread) in needle and in bobbin.

- An accurate ¼" seam allowance is *essential*. Presser feet that are ¼" wide are available for most sewing machines.

- When piecing, always place pieces right sides together and match raw edges; pin if necessary.

SEWING ACROSS SEAM INTERSECTIONS

When sewing across intersection of two seams, place pieces right sides together and match seams exactly, making sure seam allowances are pressed in opposite directions (**Fig. 4**).

Fig. 4

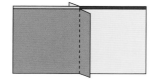

SEWING SHARP POINTS

To ensure sharp points when joining triangular pieces, stitch across the center of the "X" (shown in blue) formed on the wrong side by previous seams (**Fig. 5**).

Fig. 5

PRESSING

- Use steam iron set on "Cotton" for all pressing.

- Press after sewing each seam.

- Seam allowances are almost always pressed to one side, usually toward darker fabric. However, to reduce bulk it may occasionally be necessary to press seam allowances toward the lighter fabric or even to press them open.

- To prevent dark fabric seam allowance from showing through light fabric, trim darker seam allowance slightly narrower than lighter seam allowance.

- To press long seams without curving or other distortion, lay seams across width of the ironing board.

QUILTING

Quilting holds the three layers (top, batting, and backing) of the quilt together and can be done by hand or machine. Because marking, layering, and quilting are interrelated and may be done in different orders depending on circumstances, please read entire **Quilting** *section, pages 40-43, before beginning project.*

TYPES OF QUILTING DESIGNS

In the Ditch Quilting
Quilting along seamlines or along edges of appliquéd pieces is called "in the ditch" quilting. This type of quilting should be done on side **opposite** seam allowance and does not have to be marked.

Motif Quilting
Quilting a design, such as a feathered wreath, is called "motif" quilting. This type of quilting should be marked before basting quilt layers together.

Channel Quilting
Quilting with straight, parallel lines is called "channel" quilting. This type of quilting may be marked or stitched using a guide.

Crosshatch Quilting
Quilting straight lines in a grid pattern is called "crosshatch" quilting. Lines may be stitched parallel to edges of quilt or stitched diagonally. This type of quilting may be marked or stitched using a guide.

Meandering Quilting
Quilting in random curved lines and swirls is called "meandering" quilting. Quilting lines should not cross or touch each other. This type of quilting does not need to be marked.

MARKING QUILTING LINES
Quilting lines may be marked using fabric marking pencils, chalk markers, or water- or air-soluble pens.

Simple quilting designs may be marked with chalk or chalk pencil after basting. A small area may be marked, then quilted, before moving to next area to be marked. Intricate designs should be marked before basting using a more durable marker.

Caution: Pressing may permanently set some marks. **Test** different markers **on scrap fabric** to find one that marks clearly and can be thoroughly removed.

A wide variety of pre-cut quilting stencils, as well as entire books of quilting patterns, are available. Using a stencil makes it easier to mark intricate or repetitive designs.

To make a stencil from a pattern, center template plastic over pattern and use a permanent marker to trace pattern onto plastic. Use a craft knife with single or double blade to cut channels along traced lines (**Fig. 6**).

Fig. 6

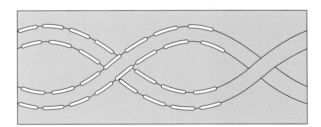

PREPARING THE BACKING

To allow for slight shifting of quilt top during quilting, backing should be approximately 4" larger on all sides. Yardage requirements listed for quilt backings are calculated for 43"/44" wide fabric. Using 90" or 108" wide fabric for the backing may eliminate piecing. To piece a backing using 43"/44" wide fabric, use the following instructions.

1. Measure length and width of quilt top; add 8" to each measurement.

2. If determined width is 79" or less, cut backing fabric into two lengths the determined *length* measurement. Trim selvages. Place lengths with right sides facing and sew long edges together, forming a tube (**Fig. 7**). Match seams and press along one fold (**Fig. 8**). Cut along pressed fold to form a single piece (**Fig. 9**).

3. If determined width is more than 79", it may require less fabric yardage if the backing is pieced horizontally. Divide determined *length* measurement by 40" to determine how many widths will be needed. Cut required number of widths the determined *width* measurement. Trim selvages. Sew long edges together to form single piece.

4. Trim backing to size determined in Step 1; press seam allowances open.

Fig. 7

Fig. 8

Fig. 9

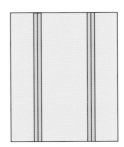

CHOOSING THE BATTING

The appropriate batting will make quilting easier. For fine hand quilting, choose low-loft batting. All cotton or cotton/polyester blend battings work well for machine quilting because the cotton helps "grip" quilt layers. If quilt is to be tied, a high-loft batting, sometimes called extra-loft or fat batting, may be used to make quilt "fluffy."

Types of batting include cotton, polyester, wool, cotton/polyester blend, cotton/wool blend, and silk.

When selecting batting, refer to package labels for characteristics and care instructions. Cut batting same size as prepared backing.

ASSEMBLING THE QUILT

1. Examine wrong side of quilt top closely; trim any seam allowances and clip any threads that may show through front of the quilt. Press quilt top, being careful not to "set" any marked quilting lines.
2. Place backing *wrong* side up on flat surface. Use masking tape to tape edges of backing to surface. Place batting on top of backing fabric. Smooth batting gently, being careful not to stretch or tear. Center quilt top *right* side up on batting.
3. Use 1" rustproof safety pins to "pin-baste" all layers together, spacing pins approximately 4" apart. Begin at center and work toward outer edges to secure all layers. If possible, place pins away from areas that will be quilted, although pins may be removed as needed when quilting.

MACHINE QUILTING METHODS

Use general-purpose thread in bobbin. Do not use quilting thread. Thread the needle with general-purpose thread or transparent monofilament thread to make quilting blend with quilt top fabrics. Use decorative thread, such as a metallic or contrasting-color general-purpose thread, to make quilting lines stand out more.

Straight-Line Quilting

The term "straight-line" is somewhat deceptive, since curves (especially gentle ones) as well as straight lines can be stitched with this technique.

1. Set stitch length for six to ten stitches per inch and attach a walking foot to sewing machine.
2. Determine which section of quilt will have the longest continuous quilting line, oftentimes the area from center top to center bottom. Roll up and secure each edge of quilt to help reduce the bulk, keeping fabrics smooth. Smaller projects may not need to be rolled.
3. Begin stitching on longest quilting line, using very short stitches for the first $1/4$" to "lock" quilting. Stitch across project, using one hand on each side of walking foot to slightly spread fabric and to guide fabric through machine. Lock stitches at end of quilting line.
4. Continue machine quilting, stitching longer quilting lines first to stabilize quilt before moving on to other areas.

Free-Motion Quilting

Free-motion quilting may be free form or may follow a marked pattern.

1. Attach a darning foot to sewing machine and lower or cover feed dogs.
2. Position quilt under darning foot; lower foot. Holding top thread, take a stitch and pull bobbin thread to top of quilt. To "lock" beginning of quilting line, hold top and bobbin threads while making three to five stitches in place.
3. Use one hand on each side of darning foot to slightly spread fabric and to move fabric through the machine. Even stitch length is achieved by using smooth, flowing hand motion and steady machine speed. Slow machine speed and fast hand movement will create long stitches. Fast machine speed and slow hand movement will create short stitches. Move quilt sideways, back and forth, in a circular motion, or in a random motion to create desired designs; do not rotate quilt. Lock stitches at end of each quilting line.

MAKING A HANGING SLEEVE

Attaching a hanging sleeve to the back of a quilt before the binding is added will allow you to display the quilt on a wall.

1. Measure width of quilt top edge and subtract 1". Cut a piece of fabric 7" wide by the determined measurement.
2. Press short edges of fabric piece $1/4$" to wrong side; press edges $1/4$" to wrong side again and machine stitch in place.
3. Matching wrong sides, fold piece in half lengthwise to form tube.
4. Follow project instructions to sew binding to quilt top and to trim backing and batting. Before Blindstitching binding to backing, match raw edges and stitch hanging sleeve to center top edge on back of quilt.
5. Finish binding quilt, treating hanging sleeve as part of backing.
6. Blindstitch bottom of hanging sleeve to backing, taking care not to stitch through to front of quilt.
7. Insert dowel or slat into hanging sleeve.

BINDING

1. Using diagonal seams (**Fig. 10**), sew binding strips together end to end.

Fig. 10

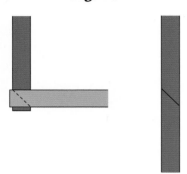

2. Matching wrong sides and raw edges, press strips in half lengthwise to complete binding.

3. Beginning with one end near center on bottom edge of quilt, lay binding around quilt to make sure that seams in binding will not end up at a corner. Adjust placement if necessary. Matching raw edges of binding to raw edge of quilt top, pin binding to right side of quilt along one edge.

4. When you reach first corner, mark ¹/₄" from corner of quilt top (**Fig. 11**).

Fig. 11

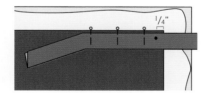

5. Beginning approximately 10" from end of binding and using ¹/₄" seam allowance, sew binding to quilt, backstitching at beginning of stitching and at mark (**Fig. 12**). Lift needle out of fabric and clip thread.

Fig. 12

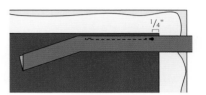

6. Fold binding as shown in **Figs. 13-14** and pin binding to adjacent side, matching raw edges. When you've reached the next corner, mark ¹/₄" from edge of quilt top.

Fig. 13

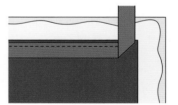

Fig. 14

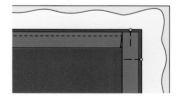

7. Backstitching at edge of quilt top, sew pinned binding to quilt (**Fig. 15**); backstitch at the next mark. Lift needle out of fabric and clip thread.

Fig. 15

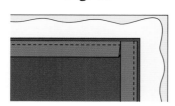

8. Continue sewing binding to quilt, stopping approximately 10" from starting point (**Fig. 16**).

Fig. 16

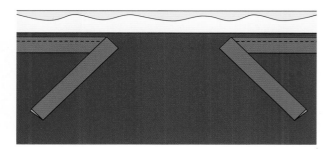

9. Bring beginning and end of binding to center of opening and fold each end back, leaving a ¹/₄" space between folds (**Fig. 17**). Finger press folds.

Fig. 17

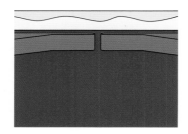

10. Unfold ends of binding and draw a line across wrong side in finger-pressed crease. Draw a line through the lengthwise pressed fold of binding at the same spot to create a cross mark. With edge of ruler at cross mark, line up 45° angle marking on ruler with one long side of binding. Draw a diagonal line from edge to edge. Repeat on remaining end, making sure that the two diagonal lines are angled the same way (**Fig. 18**).

Fig. 18

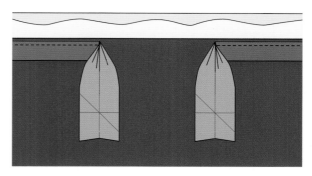

11. Matching right sides and diagonal lines, pin binding ends together at right angles (**Fig. 19**).

Fig. 19

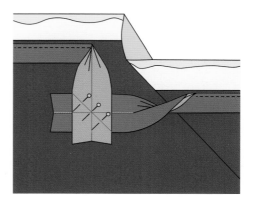

12. Machine stitch along diagonal line (**Fig. 20**), removing pins as you stitch.

Fig. 20

13. Lay binding against quilt to double check that it is correct length.
14. Trim binding ends, leaving ¼" seam allowance; press seam open. Stitch binding to quilt.
15. Trim backing and batting even with edges of quilt top.

16. On one edge of quilt, fold binding over to quilt backing and pin pressed edge in place, covering stitching line (**Fig. 21**). On adjacent side, fold binding over, forming a mitered corner (**Fig. 22**). Repeat to pin remainder of binding in place.

Fig. 21

Fig. 22

7. Blindstitch binding to backing, taking care not to stitch through to front of quilt. To Blindstitch, come up at 1, go down at 2, and come up at 3 (**Fig 23**). Length of stitches may be varied as desired.

Fig. 23

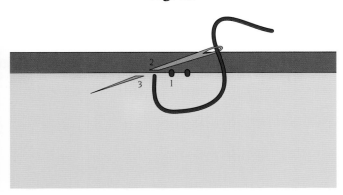

SIGNING AND DATING YOUR QUILT

A completed quilt is a work of art and should be signed and dated. There are many different ways to do this and numerous books on the subject. The label should reflect the style of the quilt, the occasion or person for which it was made, and the quilter's own particular talents. Following are suggestions for recording the history of quilt or adding a sentiment for future generations.

- Embroider quilter's name, date, and any additional information on quilt top or backing. Matching floss, such as cream floss on white border, will leave a subtle record. Bright or contrasting floss will make the information stand out.

- Make label from muslin and use permanent marker to write information. Use different colored permanent markers to make label more decorative. Stitch label to back of quilt.

- Use photo-transfer paper to add image to white or cream fabric label. Stitch label to back of quilt.

Metric Conversion Chart

Inches x 2.54 = centimeters (cm)
Inches x 25.4 = millimeters (mm)
Inches x .0254 = meters (m)

Yards x .9144 = meters (m)
Yards x 91.44 = centimeters (cm)
Centimeters x .3937 = inches (")
Meters x 1.0936 = yards (yd)

Standard Equivalents

1/8"	3.2 mm	0.32 cm	1/8 yard	11.43 cm	0.11 m
1/4"	6.35 mm	0.635 cm	1/4 yard	22.86 cm	0.23 m
3/8"	9.5 mm	0.95 cm	3/8 yard	34.29 cm	0.34 m
1/2"	12.7 mm	1.27 cm	1/2 yard	45.72 cm	0.46 m
5/8"	15.9 mm	1.59 cm	5/8 yard	57.15 cm	0.57 m
3/4"	19.1 mm	1.91 cm	3/4 yard	68.58 cm	0.69 m
7/8"	22.2 mm	2.22 cm	7/8 yard	80 cm	0.8 m
1"	25.4 mm	2.54 cm	1 yard	91.44 cm	0.91 m